STAR WARS™

DELUXE PAPER DOLLS

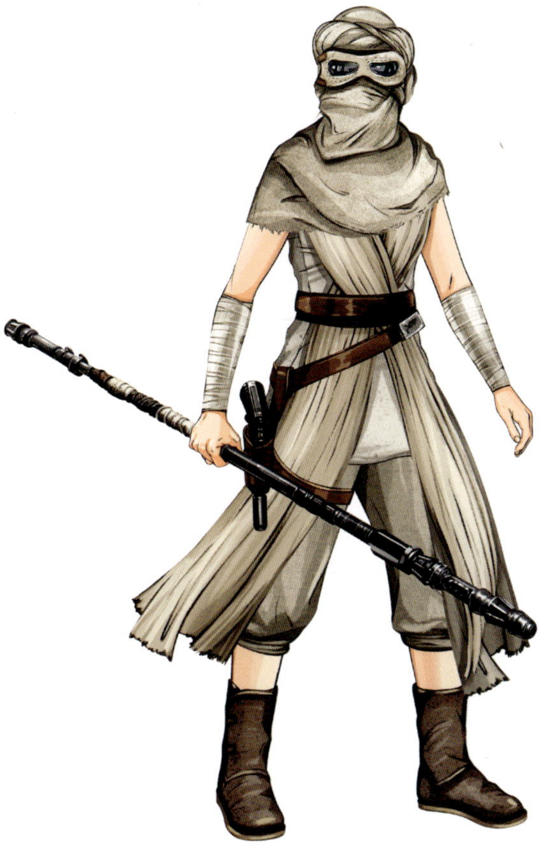

ILLUSTRATED BY NATALIA SANABRIA

WRITTEN BY STEVE BEHLING

INSIGHT EDITIONS

SAN RAFAEL • LOS ANGELES • LONDON

INSIGHT
EDITIONS
PO Box 3088
San Rafael, CA 94912
www.insighteditions.com

Find us on Facebook: www.facebook.com/InsightEditions
Follow us on Instagram: @insighteditions

ISBN: 979-8-88663-047-3

Publisher: Raoul Goff
SVP, Group Publisher: Vanessa Lopez
VP, Creative: Chrissy Kwasnik
VP, Manufacturing: Alix Nicholaeff
Editorial Director: Thom O'Hearn
Art Director: Stuart Smith
Editor: Alexis Sattler
VP, Senior Executive Project Editor: Vicki Jaeger
Managing Editor: Shannon Ballesteros
Senior Production Manager: Joshua Smith
Senior Production Manager, Subsidiary Rights: Lina s Palma-Temena

ROOTS of PEACE REPLANTED PAPER

Insight Editions, in association with Roots of Peace, will plant two trees for each tree used in the manufacturing of this book. Roots of Peace is an internationally renowned humanitarian organization dedicated to eradicating land mines worldwide and converting war-torn lands into productive farms and wildlife habitats. Roots of Peace will plant two million fruit and nut trees in Afghanistan and provide farmers there with the skills and support necessary for sustainable land use.

Manufactured in China by Insight Editions

10 9 8 7 6 5 4 3 2 1

INTRODUCTION

"A LONG TIME AGO IN A GALAXY FAR, FAR AWAY . . . ."

From the moment those words first appeared on movie screens, audiences thrilled to galactic adventures like they'd never seen before. *Star Wars* introduced our world to Luke Skywalker, Princess Leia Organa, and Han Solo, a trio of heroes fighting for the Rebellion against the evil Empire, personified by the red lightsaber-wielding Darth Vader. Their mission to free the galaxy from the Empire's tyranny took place over three films in 1977, 1980, and 1983.

But the saga was only beginning.

In 1999, writer/director/visionary George Lucas returned to tell the story of what came before the original trilogy. Dubbed "the prequel trilogy," the three movies released in 1999, 2002, and 2005 gave us the backstory of Darth Vader: his early years as Anakin Skywalker (father to Luke and Leia), his first meeting and eventual romance with Padmé Amidala (Luke and Leia's mother), and his friendship-turned-everlasting-enmity with Jedi Knight Obi-Wan Kenobi.

The Skywalker Saga, as it has come to be called, continued in another trilogy, starting with 2015's *Star Wars: The Force Awakens*. We met the mysterious Rey and stormtrooper Finn, both of whom joined the Resistance against the First Order, a tyrannical movement born from the ashes of the Empire.

Now it's time to heed the hero's call and enter an incredible galaxy of paper dolls featuring some of the most iconic characters from the *Star Wars* saga. You'll encounter their most recognized looks from the trilogies, along with alternate outfits and accessories. In addition, you'll find behind-the-scenes trivia and fun facts about the *Star Wars* cast and costume designers.

It's time to turn the page—may the Force be with you . . . .

INSTRUCTIONS

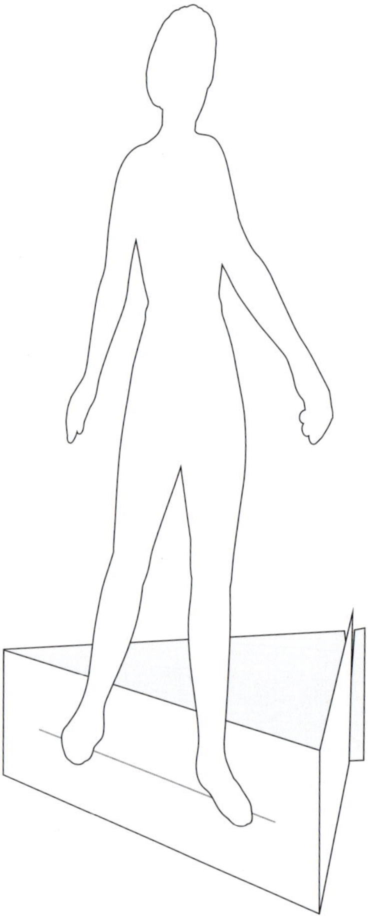

To display the dolls, carefully punch out the stand that accompanies each character. Fold each stand along the fold lines so the stand forms a triangle and then attach the two end flaps. Glue the back of the paper doll's feet to the front of the stand.

For the background scenes, carefully cut out each scene from the front and back covers. Insert the bottom of each scene into the display stands provided in the final two pages of the book. The cover can also be removed from the book to create a background pattern.

LUKE SKYWALKER

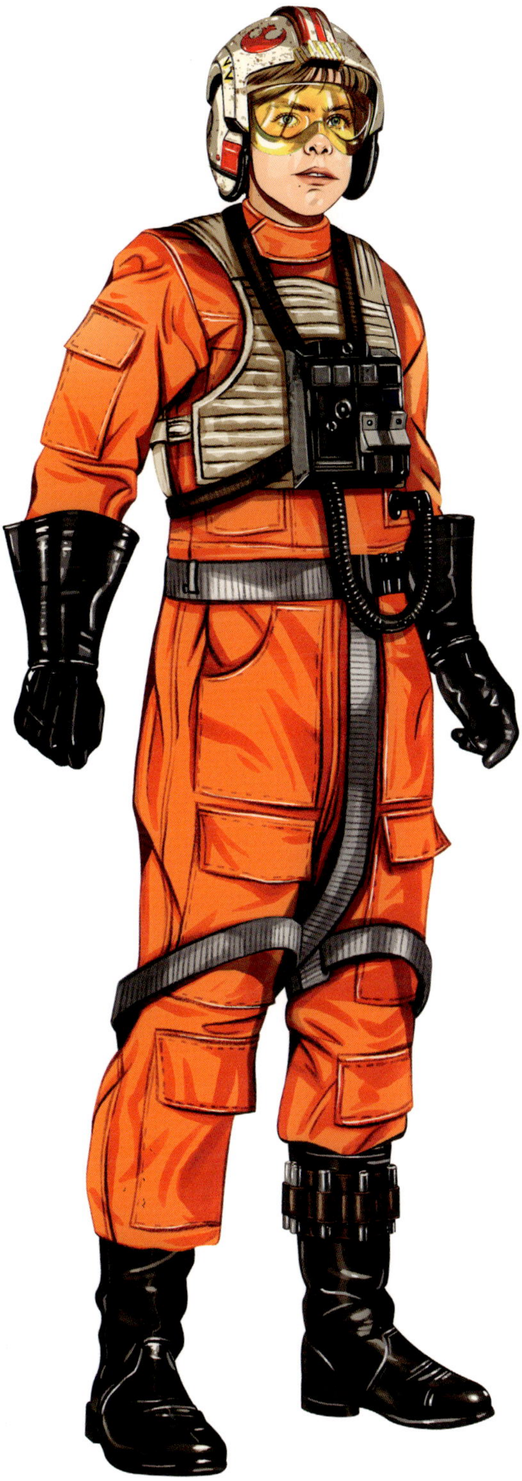

"Red Five standing by!"

LUKE SKYWALKER
Star Wars: A New Hope (1977)

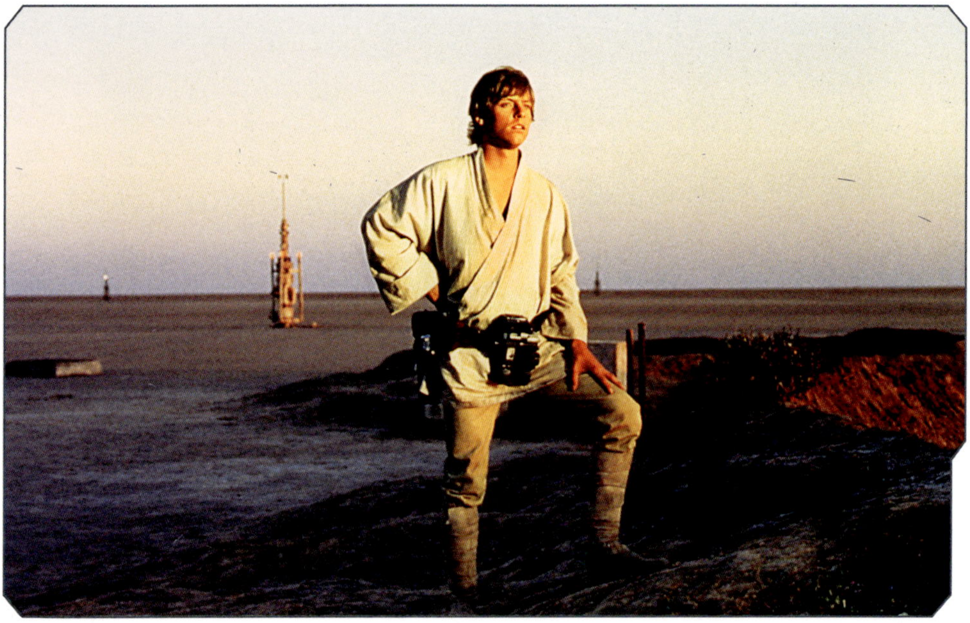

When we first encounter Mark Hamill as Luke Skywalker in 1977's *Star Wars: A New Hope*, the young man is clad in the clothes of a moisture farmer on the desert planet Tatooine. Yearning for excitement and a connection to his past, Luke soon becomes embroiled in the Rebellion against the evil Galactic Empire. Thus begins a decades-long saga told across multiple movies, television series, and transmedia content.

Over the course of the original trilogy (1977–1983), Luke evolves from a callow youth to an experienced rebel commander and, ultimately, to a full-fledged Jedi Knight. The wardrobe for the character had to reflect those various stages. But George Lucas had another caveat for costume designer John Mollo. "He didn't want anyone to notice the costumes," Mollo said. "By this, [Lucas] meant that he wanted the costumes to look real." From the practical simplicity of Luke's desert-inspired Tatooine garb to the utilitarian nature of his X-wing starfighter flight suit, the wardrobe has a lived-in feel that helps ground the fantastical elements of the films.

Mollo worked as the costume designer for *Star Wars: A New Hope* (1977) and *Star Wars: The Empire Strikes Back* (1980). For Luke's appearance in the next movie, *Star Wars: Return of the Jedi* (1983), costume designers Aggie Guerard Rodgers and Nilo Rodis-Jamero were tasked with creating Luke's Jedi look. The all-black outfit echoed the appearance of Luke's father, the ominous Darth Vader, down to the black glove the young Jedi wore on his cybernetic right hand.

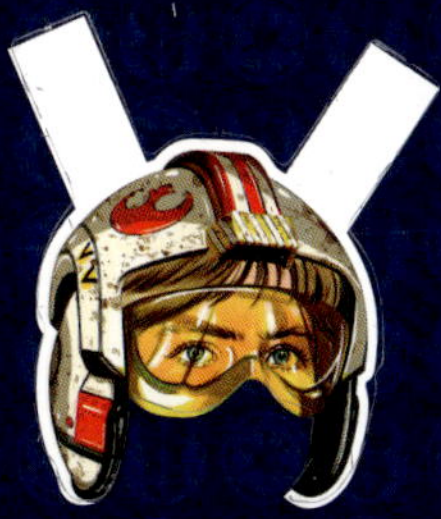

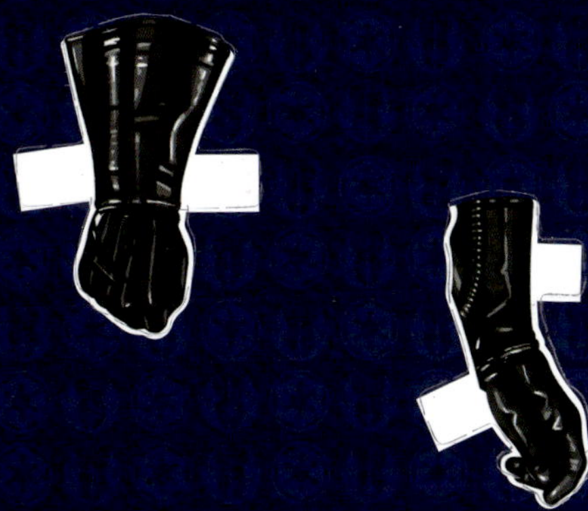

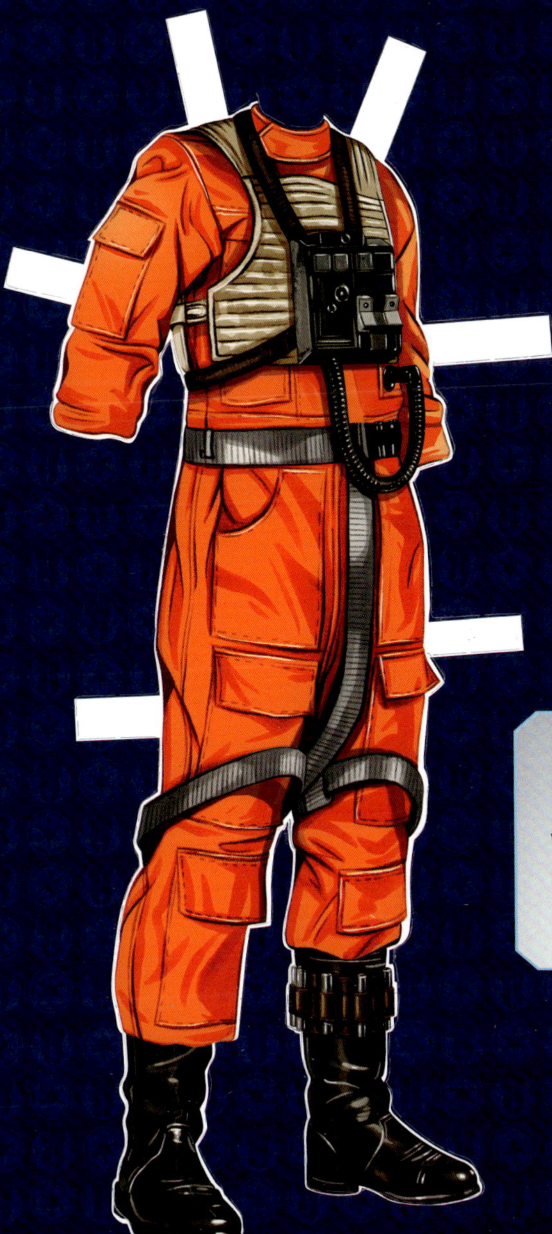

The iconic orange flight suits worn by rebel pilots at the climax of *Star Wars: A New Hope* were provided by a UK company called Jays Racewear. The suits are meant to recall the look of real-world fighter pilots.

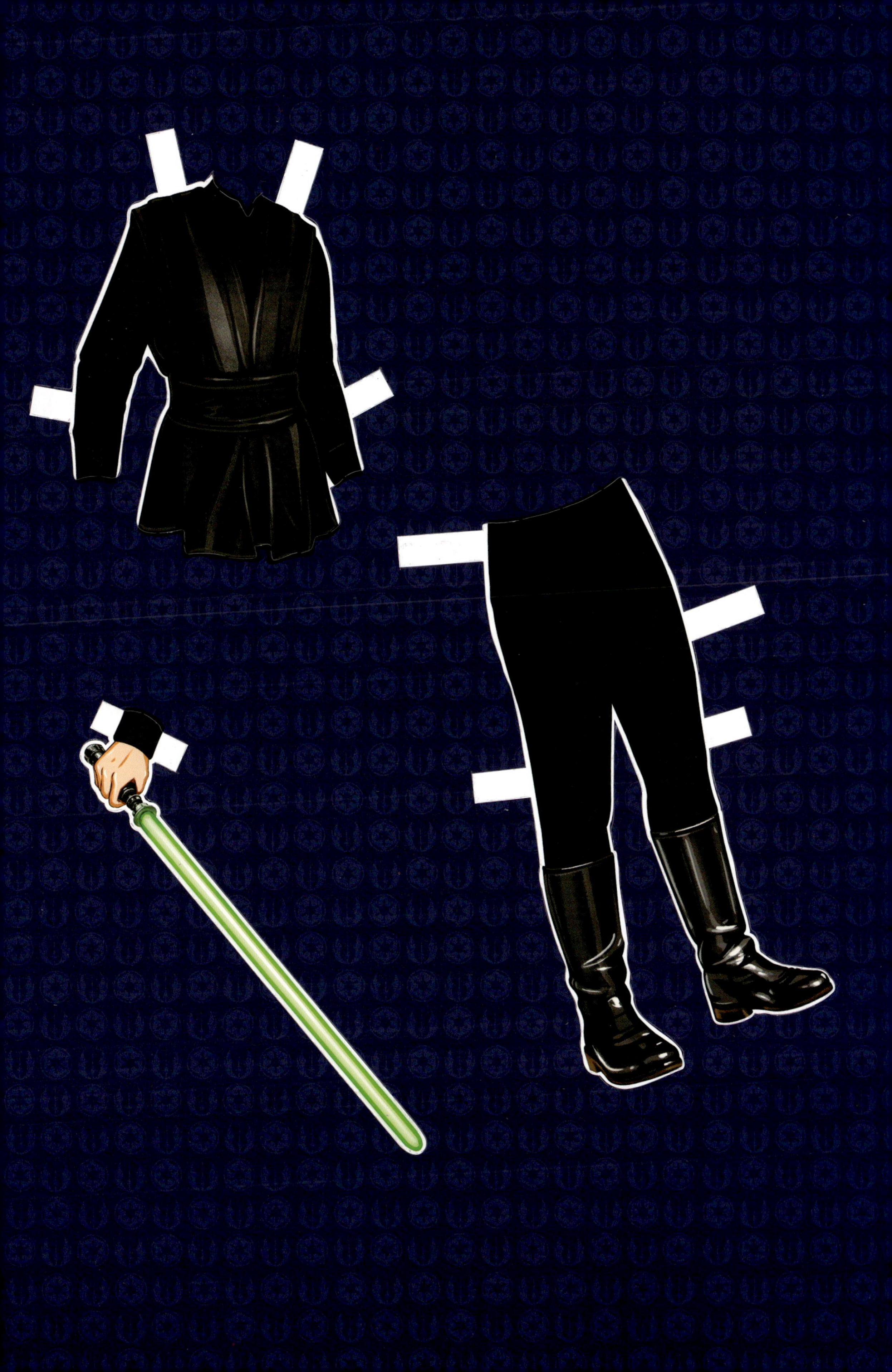

HAN SOLO

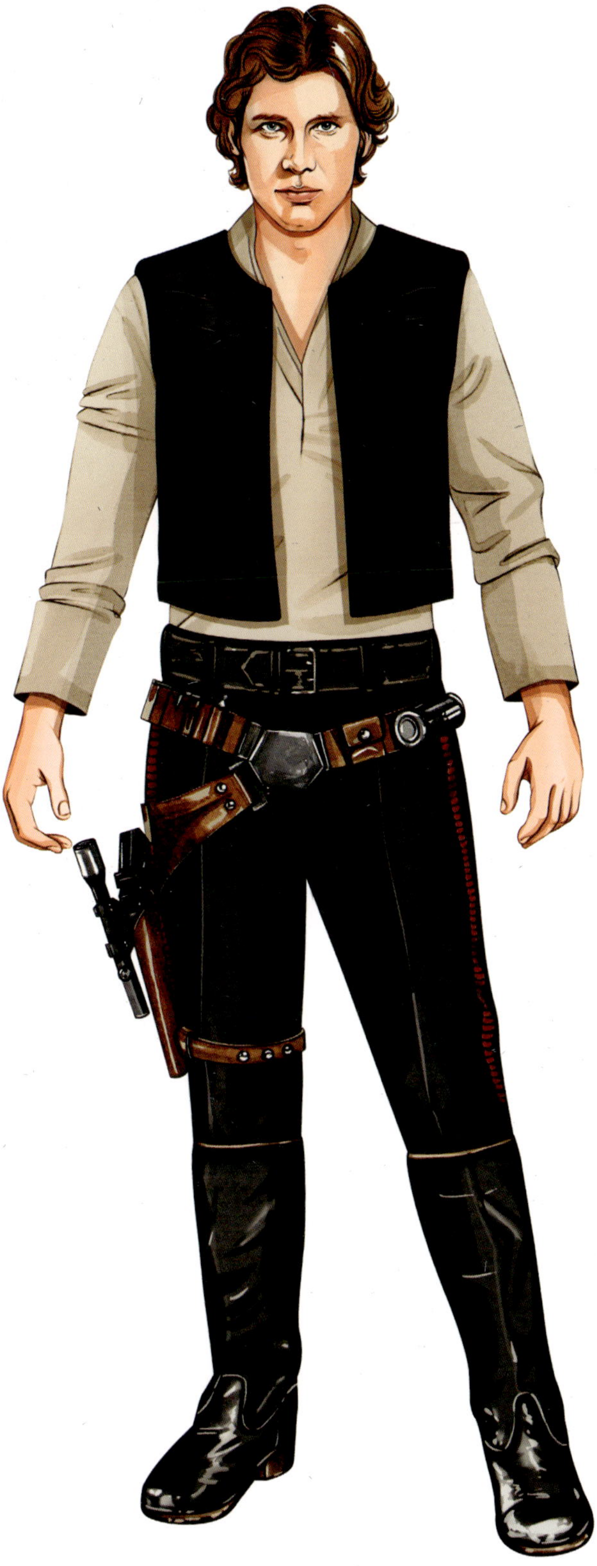

"Not a bad bit of rescuing, huh? You know, sometimes I amaze even myself."

HAN SOLO
Star Wars: A New Hope (1977)

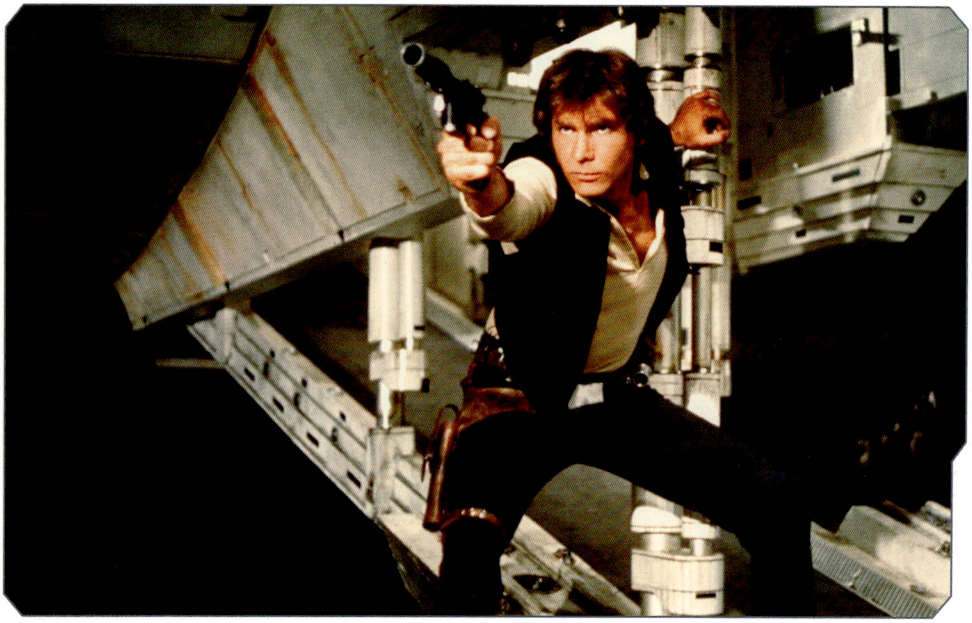

Devil-may-care smuggler Han Solo, captain of the Corellian freighter the *Millennium Falcon* ("It's the ship that made the Kessel Run in less than 12 parsecs!"), appears to be an enigma. Possessed of a grounded nature and a dry sense of humor, Han can be likened to a protagonist from a classic movie Western. The approach to his wardrobe reflects that element of his character from the moment he first meets Luke Skywalker and Obi-Wan Kenobi on Tatooine. Han's light-colored shirt, balanced against a dark vest and pants, visually illustrates the character's dichotomy—a scoundrel with the heart of a true hero. This defining look inspired and informed his base layers in the next two films, *Star Wars: The Empire Strikes Back* (1980) and *Star Wars: Return of the Jedi* (1983).

Harrison Ford had an interesting journey with the parka that Han only briefly wears on the ice planet Hoth. The brown jacket—which read as blue onscreen—was originally intended to be worn only in scenes filmed on a soundstage in England. But when production decided to take advantage of snowy conditions in Norway, where the crew was filming exterior Hoth scenes, Ford was handed his costume and instructed to hop a flight. After a long day and night of travel via plane and train, he found himself standing out in the elements in whiteout blizzard conditions. The weather was so intense that the crew filmed him from a camera positioned inside the doorway of their hotel while the actor stood out in the snow. "There I was in the middle of nowhere," Ford recalled, "with a costume that was built for the stage."

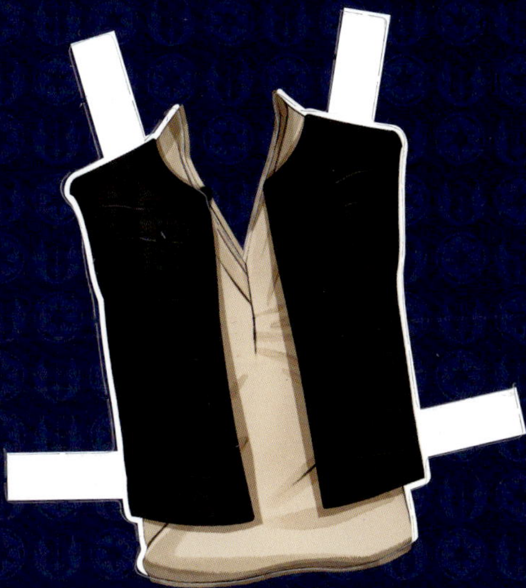

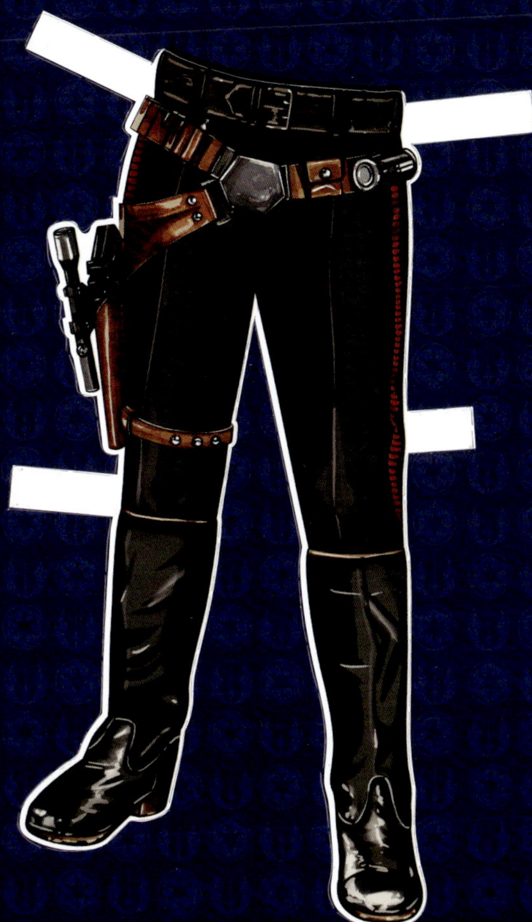

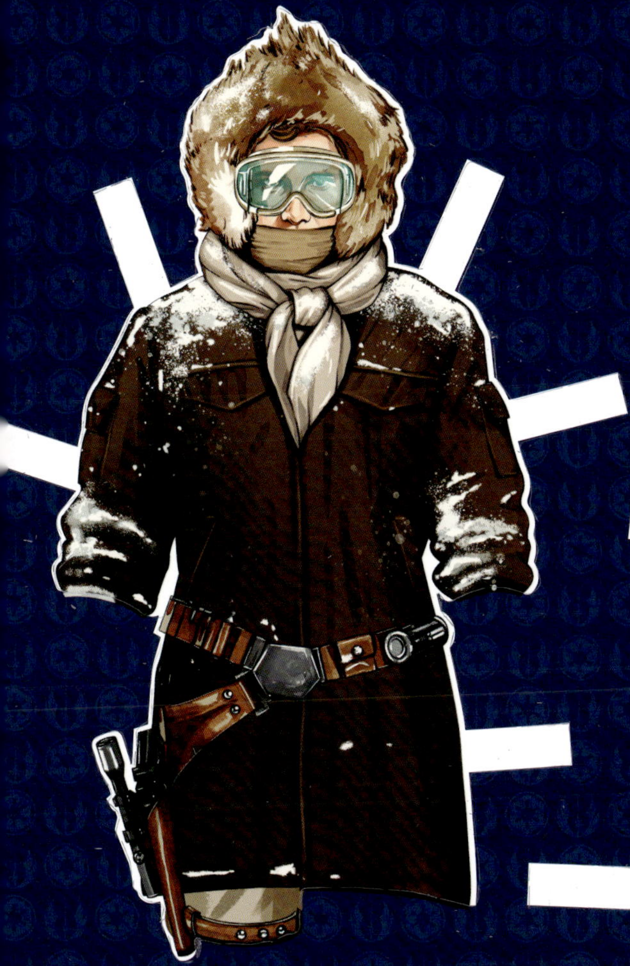

"I thought they smelled bad on the outside!"

HAN SOLO

Star Wars: The Empire Strikes Back (1980)

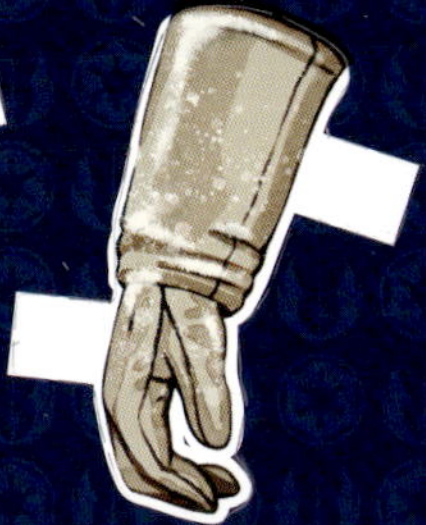

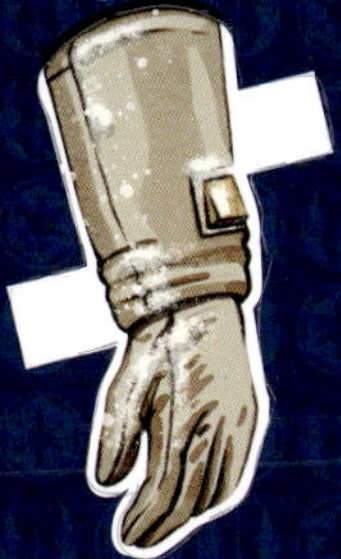

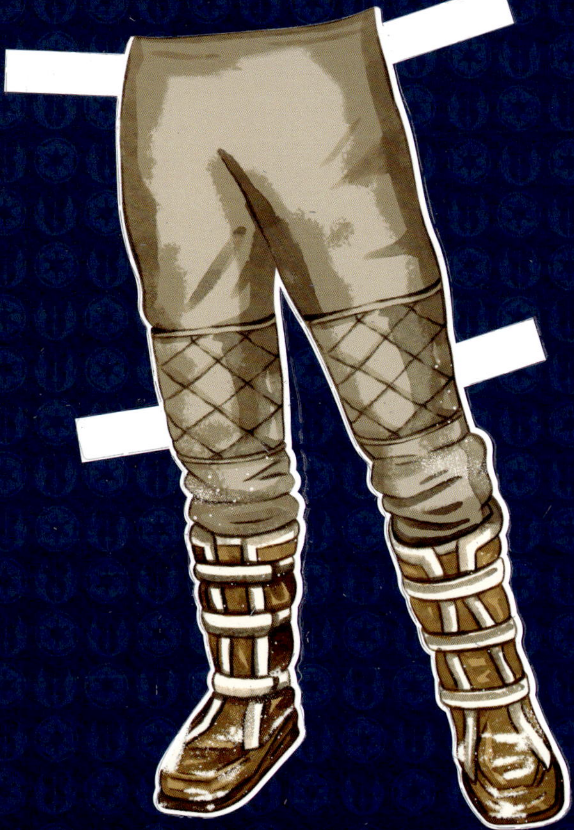

PRINCESS LEIA ORGANA

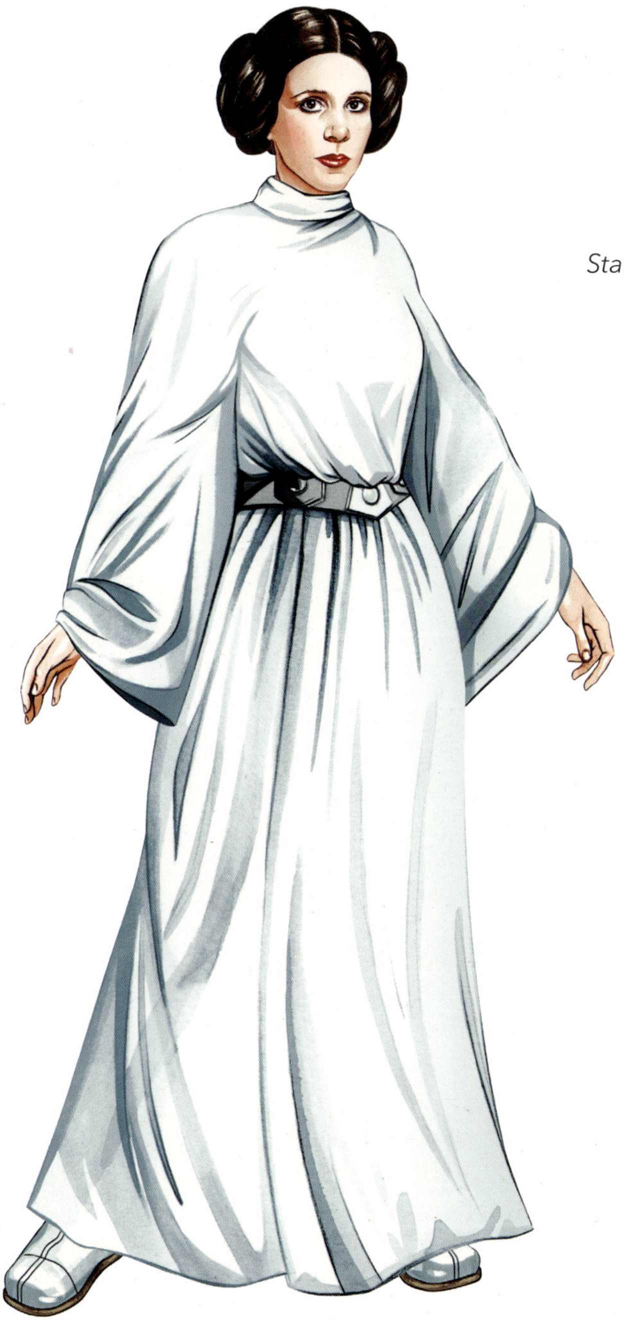

"Someone has to save our skins."

PRINCESS LEIA
Star Wars: A New Hope (1977)

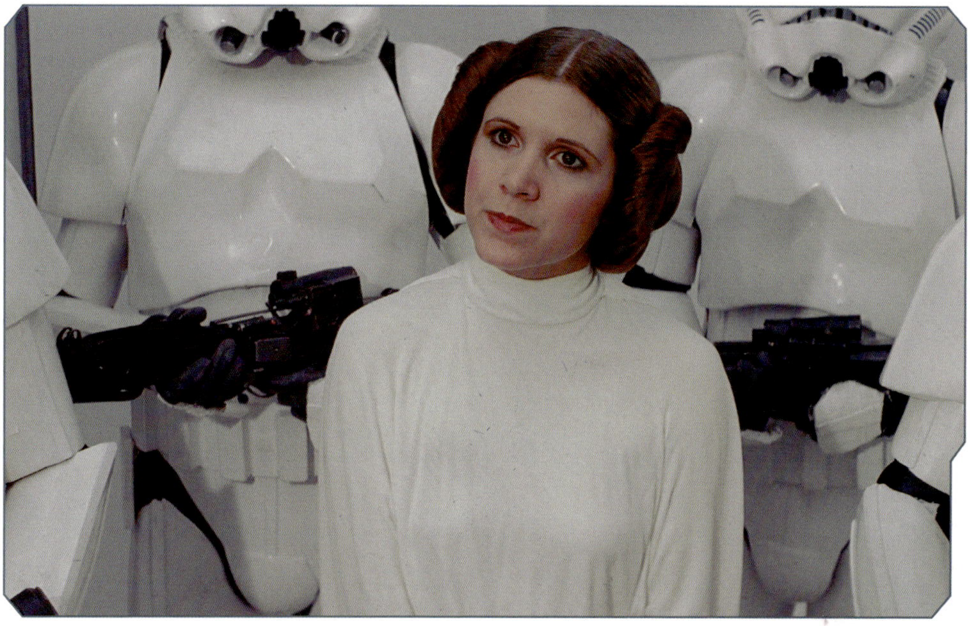

A vision in white, the daring Princess Leia Organa of Alderaan refuses to flinch in the face of evil, making her a beloved icon over the course of six *Star Wars* films. Whether she is standing up to the tyrannical Darth Vader, blasting away at stormtroopers, or directing the efforts to defeat the First Order as a general for the Resistance, Princess Leia symbolizes unwavering bravery and determination, combined with an almost effortless grace.

Throughout the films' progression, Princess Leia continues to provide the leadership needed for the rebels to overcome the sinister forces of the Empire. Leia wears a flowing white dress in *Star Wars: A New Hope* that was "broken down" before filming–that is, the character's wardrobe was physically aged to give it a well-worn look. Leia adopts an Arctic look in *Star Wars: The Empire Strikes Back* while leading the defense of the rebel base on the ice planet Hoth. Notably, that outfit is also mostly white, echoing her wardrobe in the first film. But in *Star Wars: Return of the Jedi*, Leia dons fatigues during a desperate mission to knock out a shield generator on the Forest Moon of Endor, where she engages in direct combat against the enemy.

For Leia's Endor uniform, the princess wears the same combat fatigues as those of her fellow Rebel Alliance troops. She also wears a poncho featuring camouflage details that artist Edwina Pellikka air-brushed onto white fabric. "The colors that we used really worked," Pellikka explained. "The green camouflage was this sort of lime green, and then a darker green, and a fawn color."

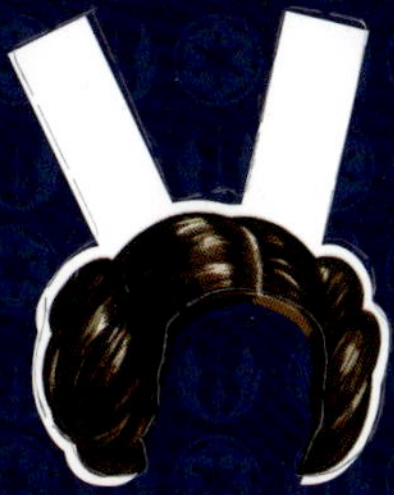

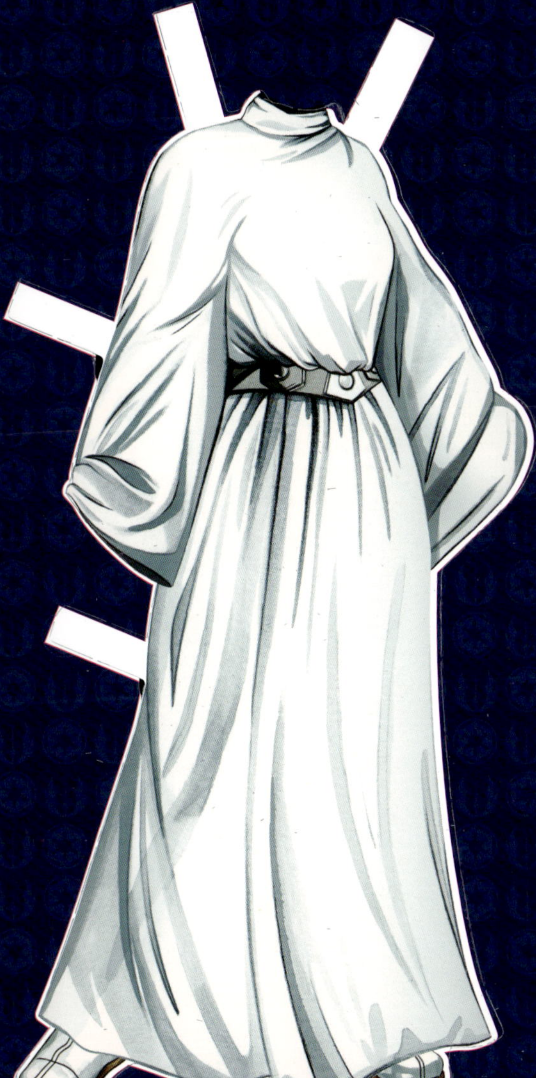

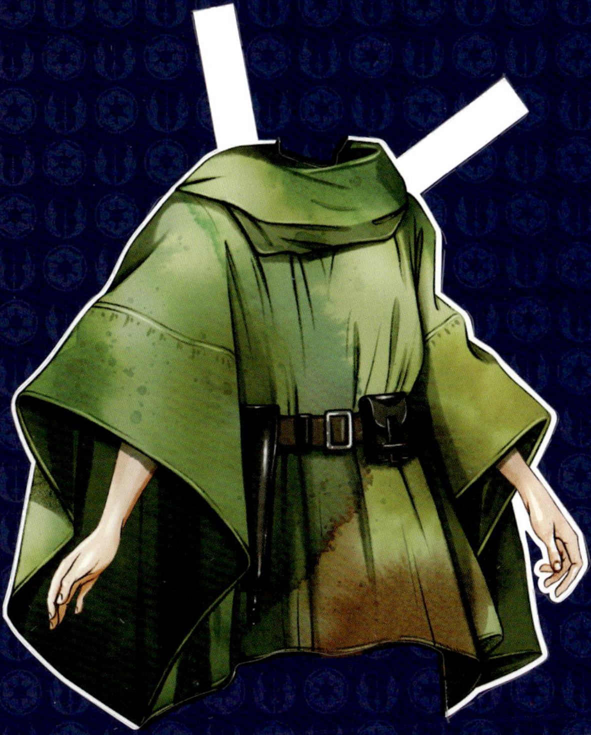

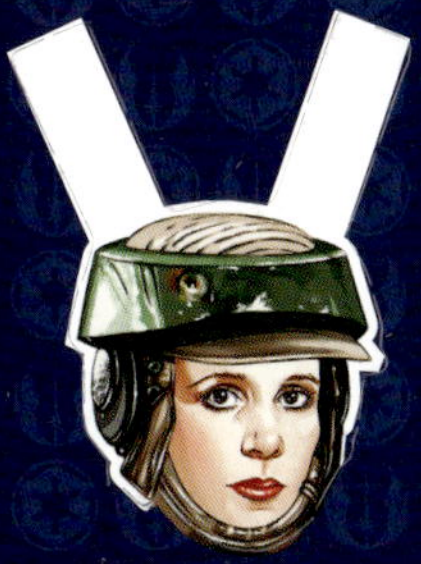

"Look, it's a hat. It's not going to hurt you."

PRINCESS LEIA

Star Wars: Return of the Jedi (1983)

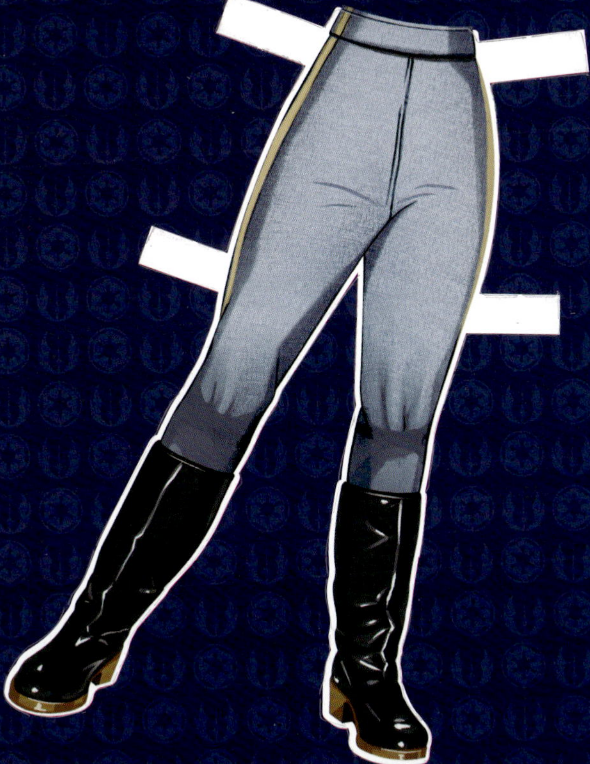

ANAKIN SKYWALKER

"Someday, I will be the most powerful Jedi ever."

ANAKIN SKYWALKER
Star Wars: Attack of the Clones
(2002)

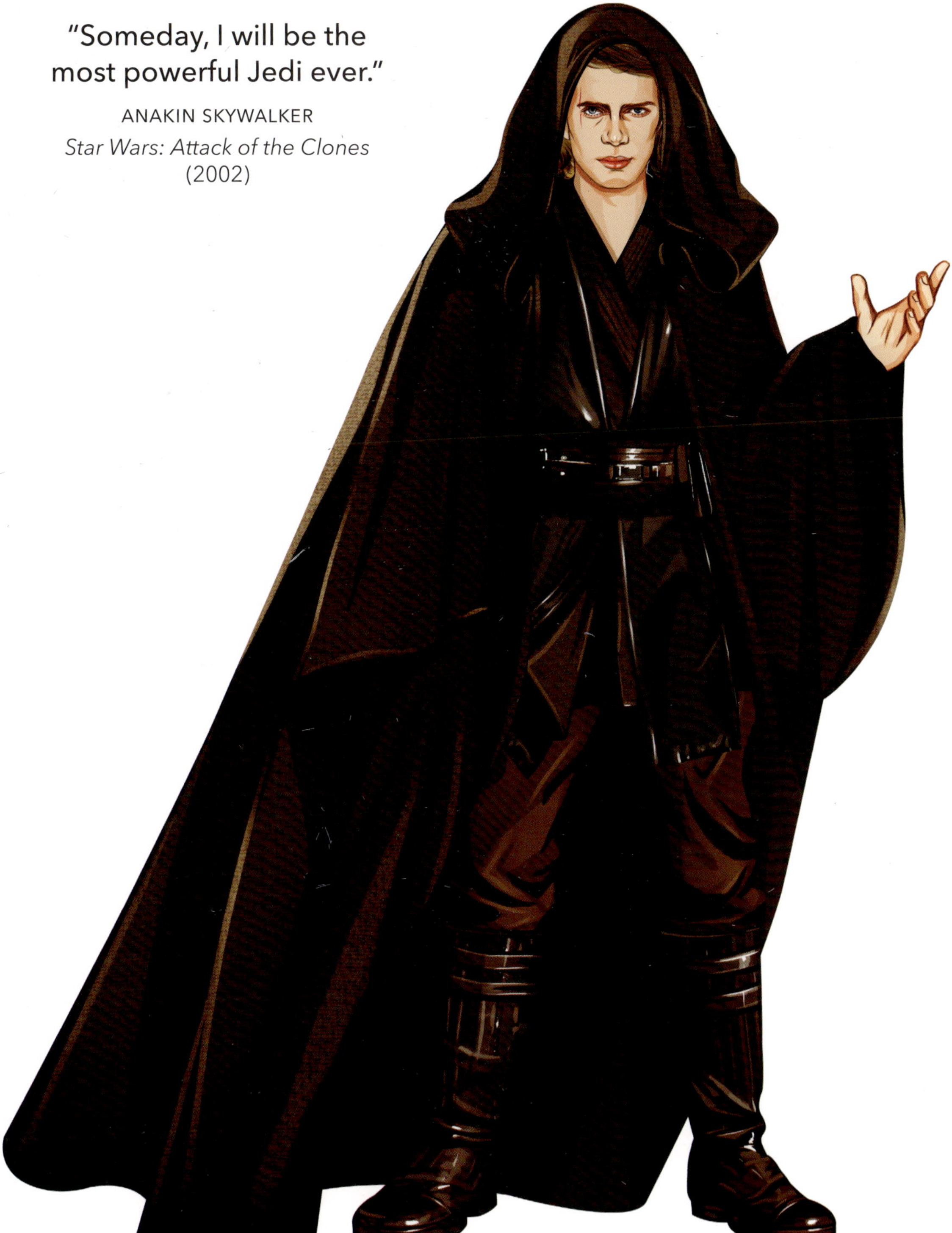

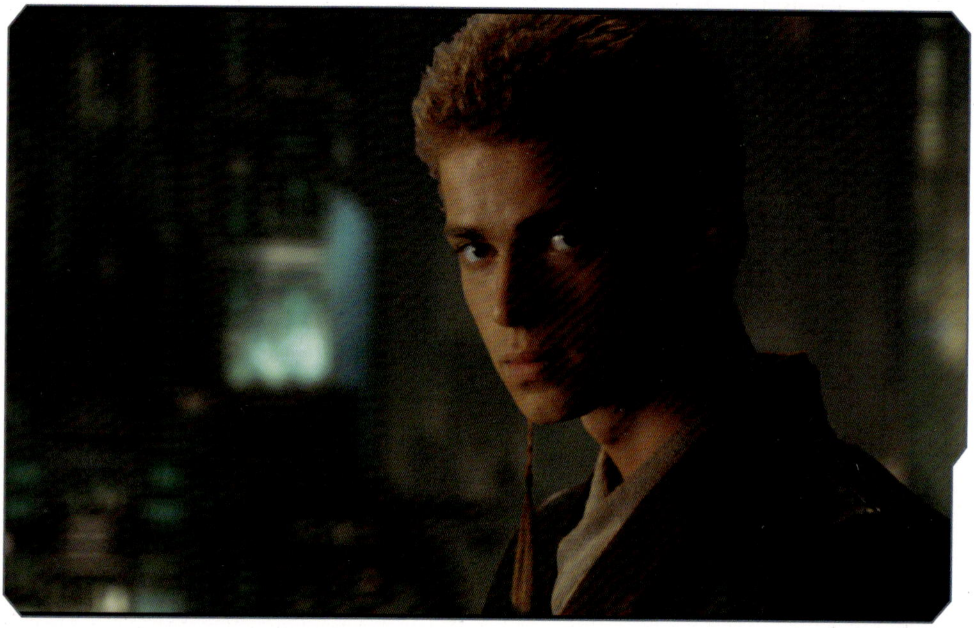

A working actor since childhood, Hayden Christensen was nineteen years old and living with a roommate in an apartment in Vancouver, Canada, when he got the call that he'd landed the role of Anakin Skywalker in *Star Wars: Attack of the Clones* (2002) and *Star Wars: Revenge of the Sith* (2005). But before Christensen played the part, audiences were introduced to a young Anakin Skywalker (portrayed by Jake Lloyd) in 1999's *Star Wars: The Phantom Menace*. The action in *Star Wars: Attack of the Clones* takes place ten years later, with Anakin now the Padawan of Jedi Knight Obi-Wan Kenobi. As Anakin edges closer to the dark side of the Force, approaching his eventual transformation into Darth Vader, the costuming also grows darker.

When Anakin eventually gives in to the dark side, he assumes a new name, Darth Vader, and adopts an ominous appearance known to moviegoers around the world. Christensen wore the fearsome suit for the first time at the end of *Star Wars: Revenge of the Sith*, a costume that John Mollo originally created for *Star Wars: A New Hope* (1977). Seventeen years passed before Christensen once more donned the imposing black suit in the Disney+ series *Obi-Wan Kenobi* (2022).

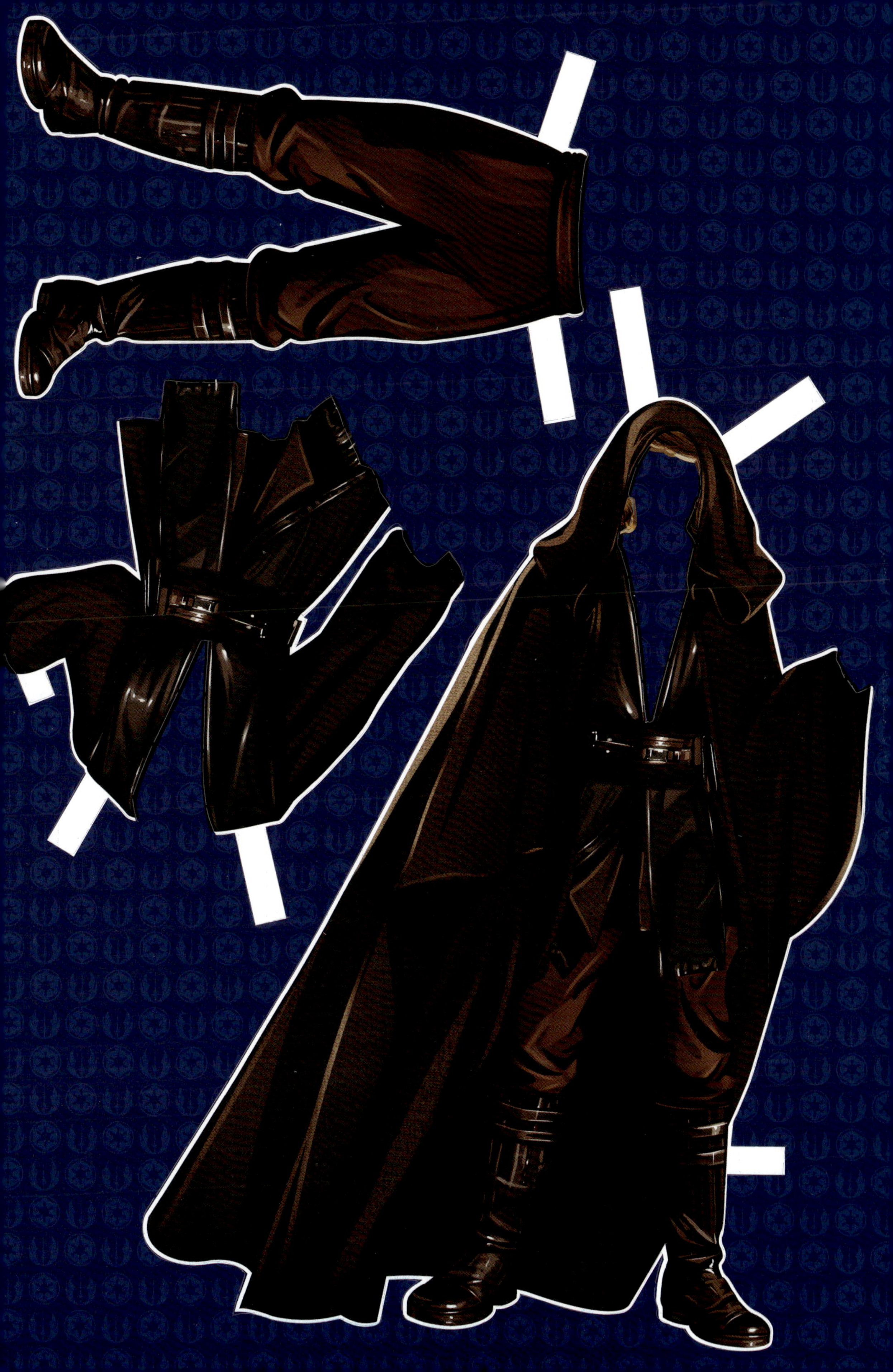

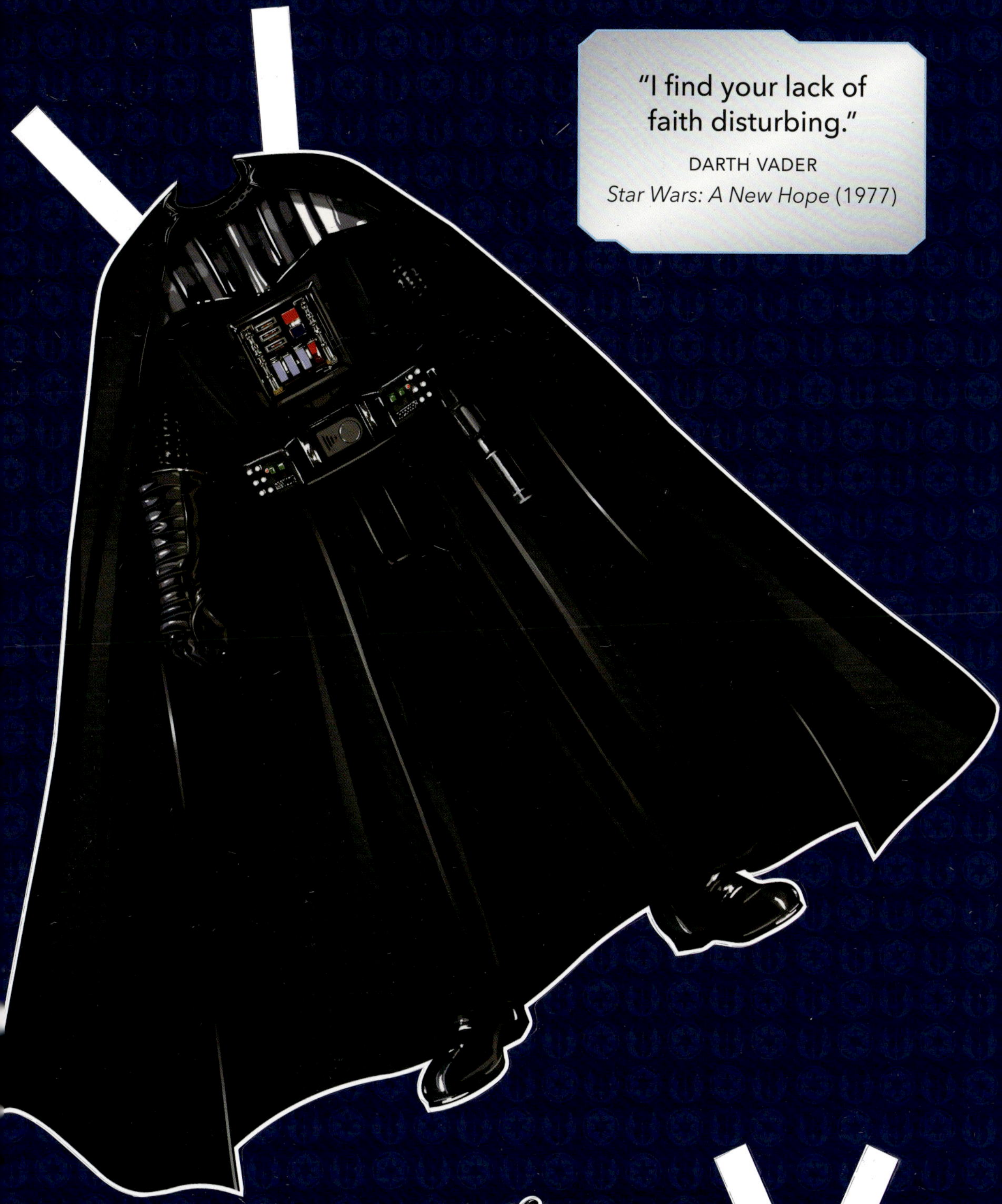

"I find your lack of faith disturbing."

DARTH VADER

Star Wars: A New Hope (1977)

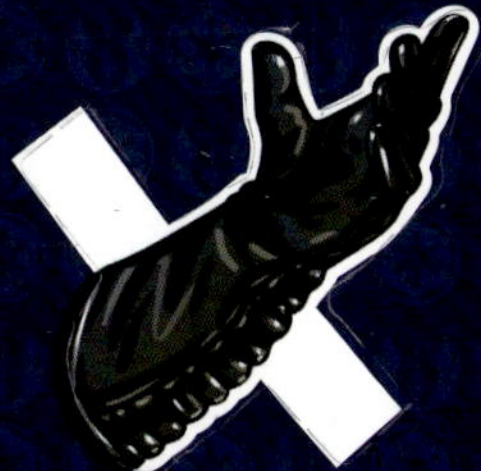

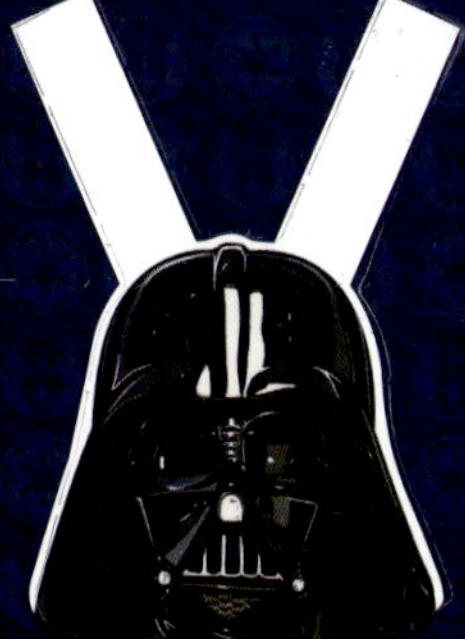

PADMÉ AMIDALA

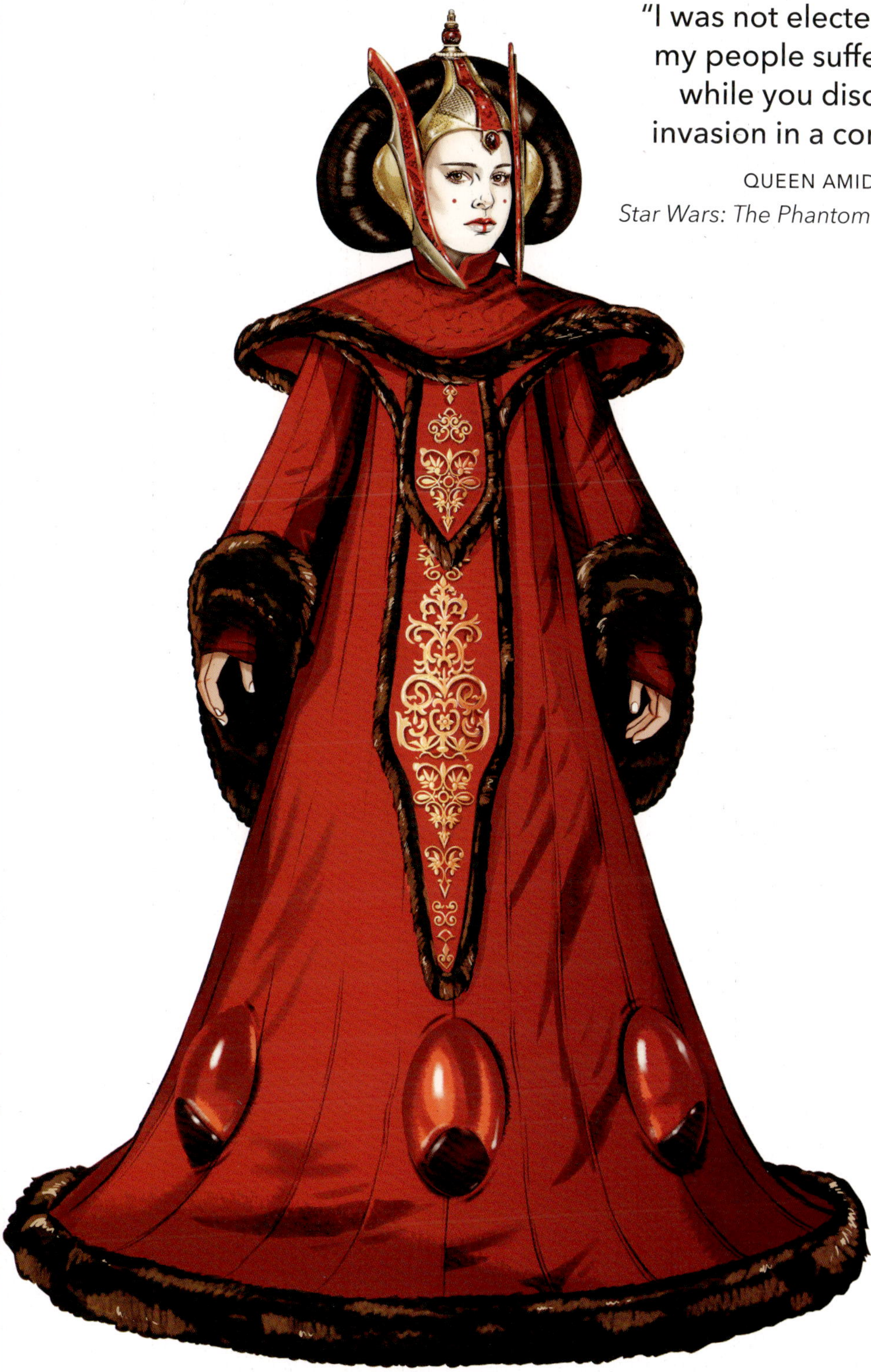

"I was not elected to watch my people suffer and die while you discuss this invasion in a committee!"

QUEEN AMIDALA
Star Wars: The Phantom Menace (1999)

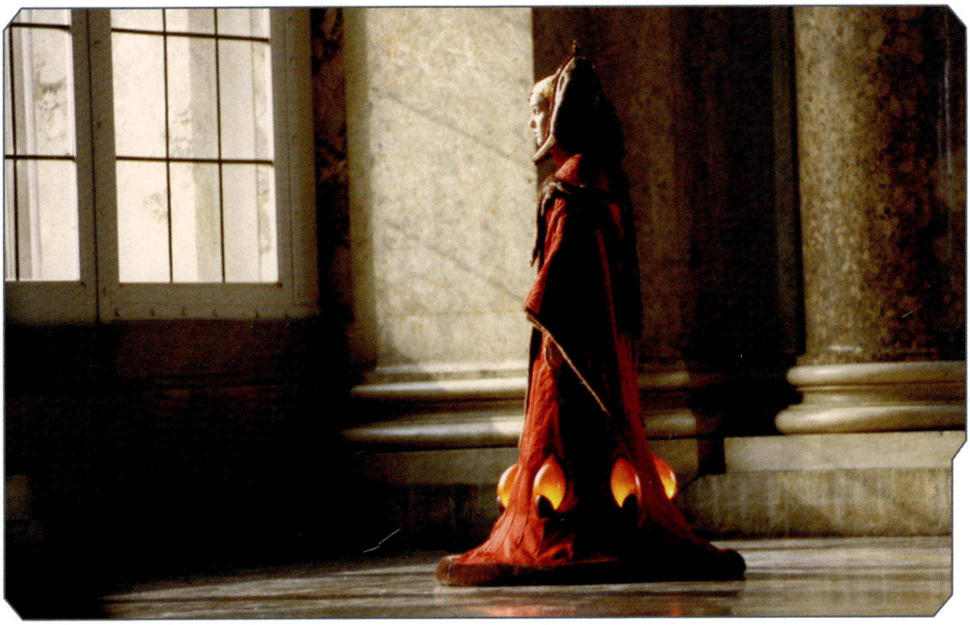

To do justice to Padmé Amidala, the queen of the planet Naboo, costume designer Trisha Biggar and her colleagues had to come up with multiple looks for the regal woman who would become a Galactic Senator and the future mother of the original trilogy's Princess Leia and Luke Skywalker. "We tried to reflect the confines and constraints of protocol and ceremonial customs in the highly detailed costumes," said Biggar, who worked on all three of the prequel films. "[They] embraced the idea of there being a dress code and a precise decorative style."

That royal look and feeling was prominently displayed in *Star Wars: The Phantom Menace*, with Padmé wearing her royal clothes as queen and also going incognito to accompany Jedi Knight Qui-Gon Jinn and his apprentice, Obi-Wan Kenobi, to Tatooine.

The costumes Padmé Amidala wears continue to reflect the character's cinematic journey throughout the trilogy. The outfits had to express her royal status as Queen of Naboo, her later station as Galactic Senator, and everything in between. According to Biggar, actress Natalie Portman wore nearly a dozen different outfits in *Star Wars: The Phantom Menace*, even though the original plan called for far fewer outfits. "By the time the script was finalized," Biggar said, "George [Lucas's] desire to expand the fashion universe had led to an almost threefold increase." The character's story is virtually told through costume, with Padmé's progression from queen to mother played out over the course of the prequels.

The throne room gown worn by Queen Amidala in *Star Wars: The Phantom Menace* began its life with an undergarment that looked like an upside-down ice cream cone.

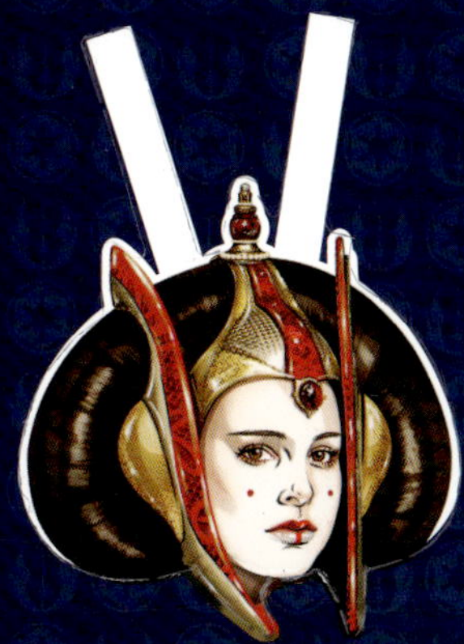

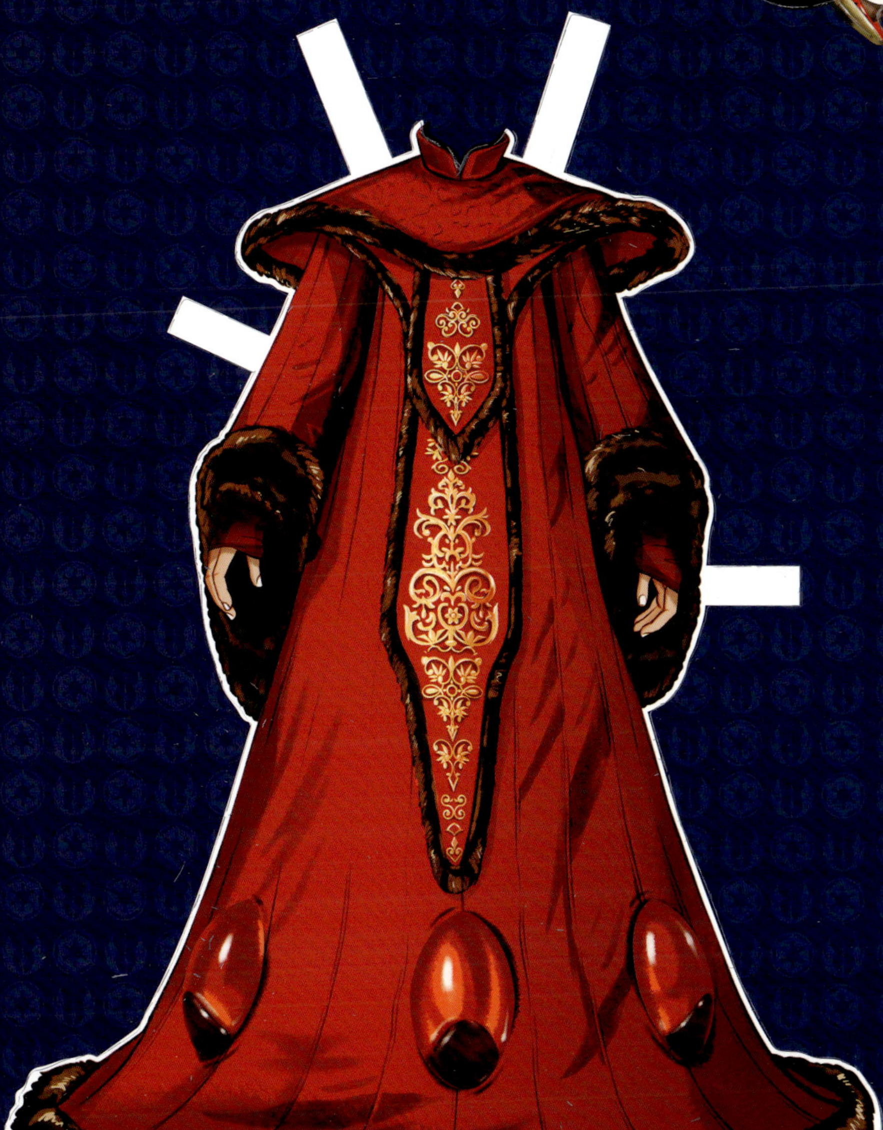

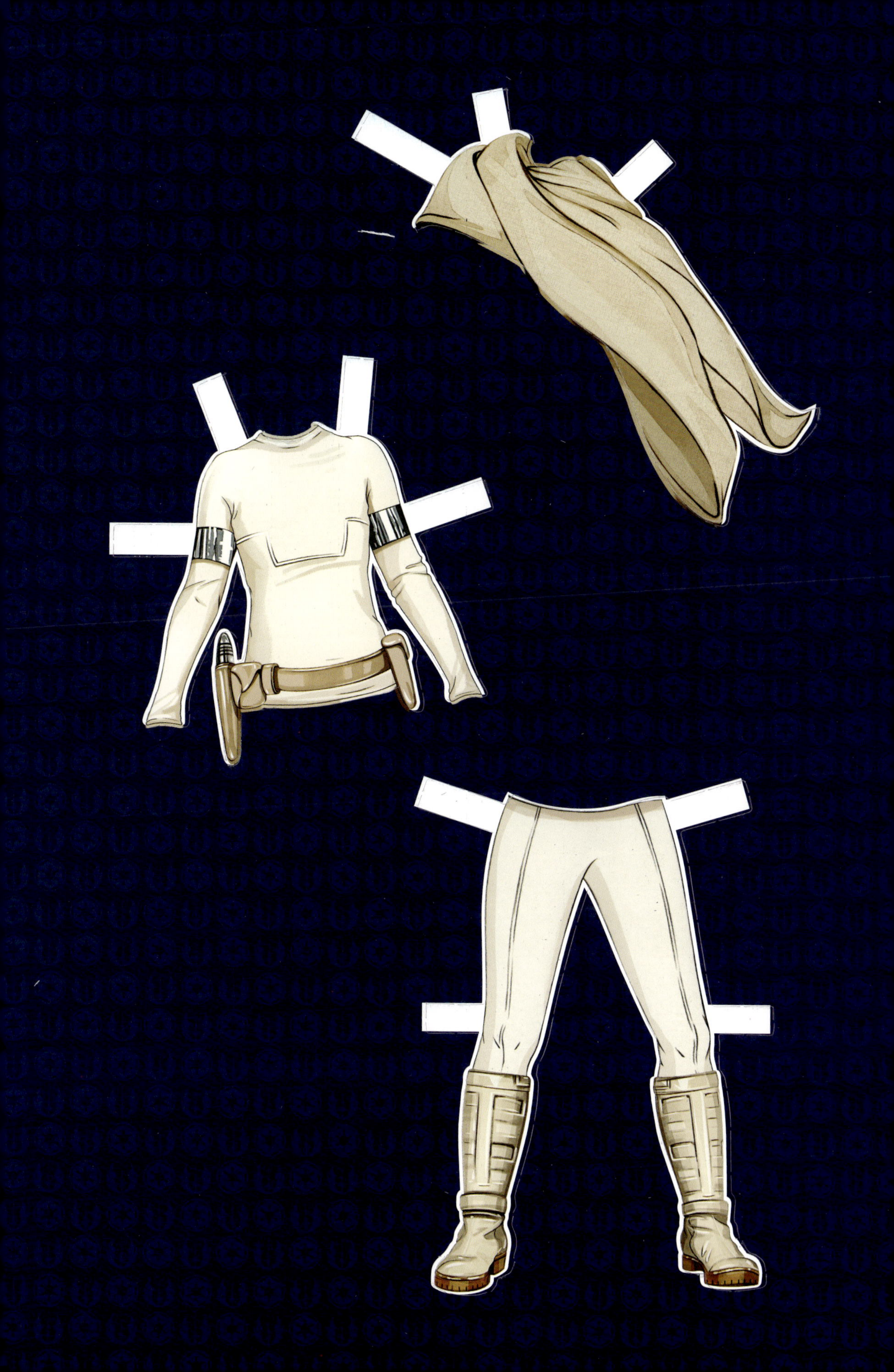

OBI-WAN KENOBI

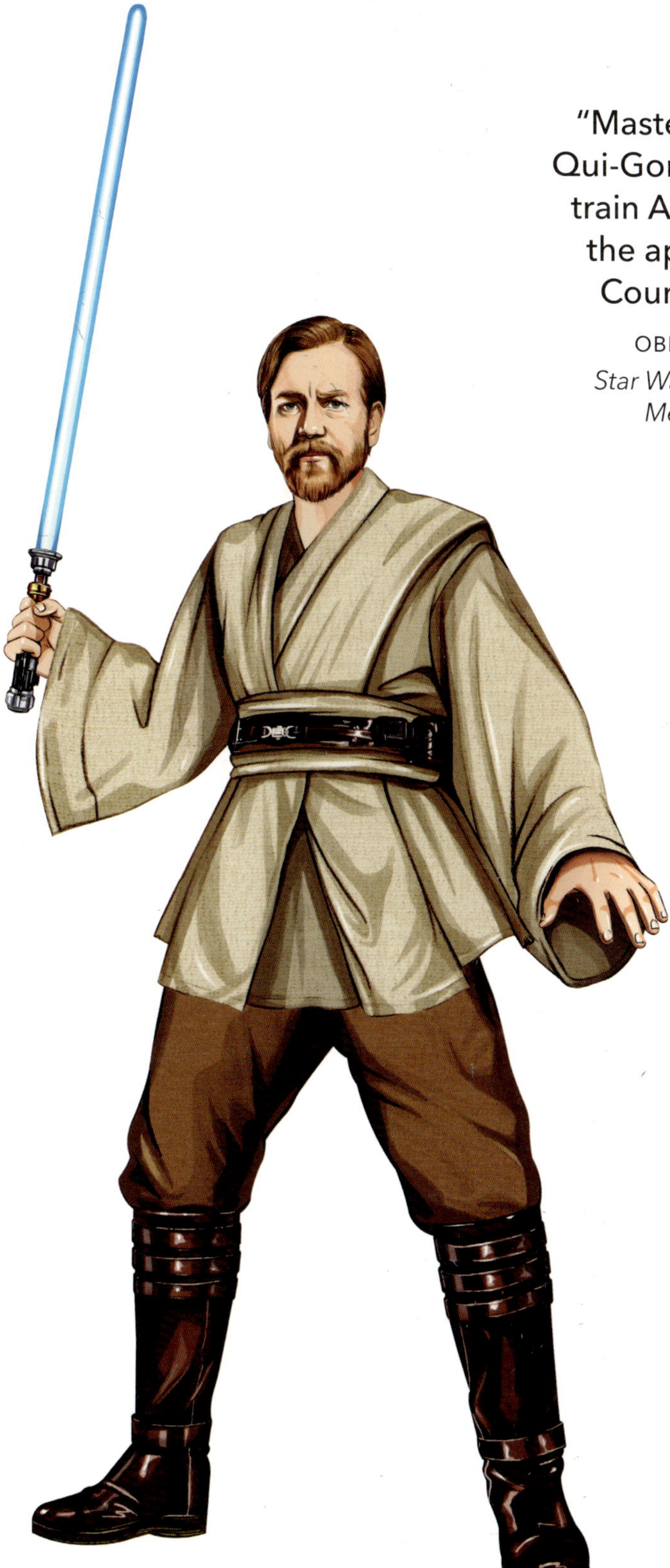

"Master Yoda, I gave Qui-Gon my word. I will train Anakin. Without the approval of the Council if I must."

OBI-WAN KENOBI

Star Wars: The Phantom Menace (1999)

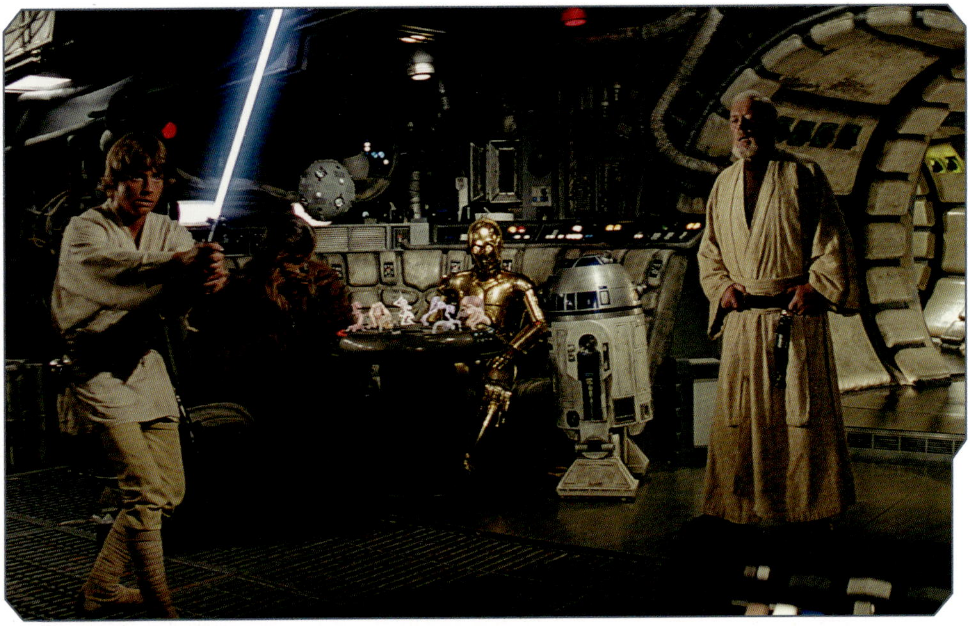

Audiences were introduced to Obi-Wan Kenobi in *Star Wars: A New Hope* (1977). Portrayed by award-winning actor Alec Guinness, the seasoned Jedi Knight is Luke Skywalker's wise mentor who teaches him the ways of the Force. When a *Star Wars* prequel trilogy was announced, the filmmakers sought someone to play a young Obi-Wan. Enter Ewan McGregor, who first saw *Star Wars: A New Hope* with his brother at the age of six. McGregor was the perfect actor to play young Obi-Wan in *Star Wars: The Phantom Menace* (1999).

Costume designer John Mollo described the challenge of creating Obi-Wan's look in *Star Wars: A New Hope*: "George [Lucas] wanted him to look part monk and part Samurai warrior," Mollo said. When it came time to work on the prequels featuring the young Obi-Wan, costume designer Trisha Biggar tracked down vintage fabric from a warehouse in London, England, that was "almost a perfect match to Alec Guinness's costume," she said. "We managed to squeeze out ten or eleven cloaks [for Ewan McGregor]."

In 2022, McGregor reprised his role in the Disney+ series *Obi-Wan Kenobi*, which takes place after *Star Wars: Revenge of the Sith*, when the Jedi are all but destroyed, and before *Star Wars: A New Hope*. Obi-Wan appears in the series as a broken man who eventually must confront his former friend and pupil, Darth Vader.

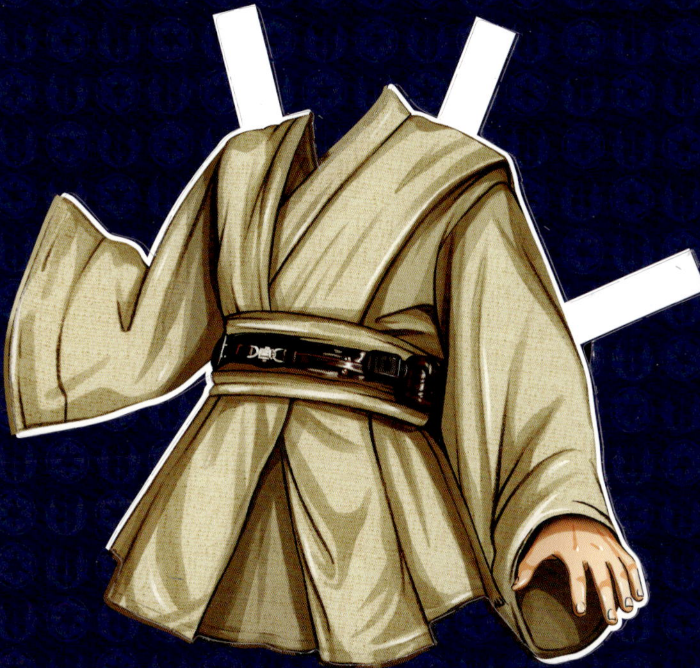

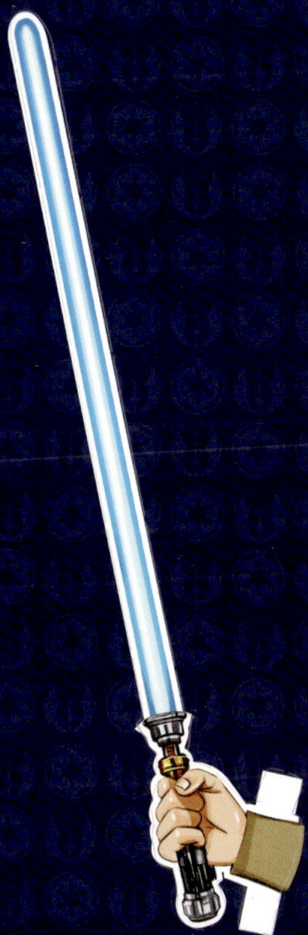

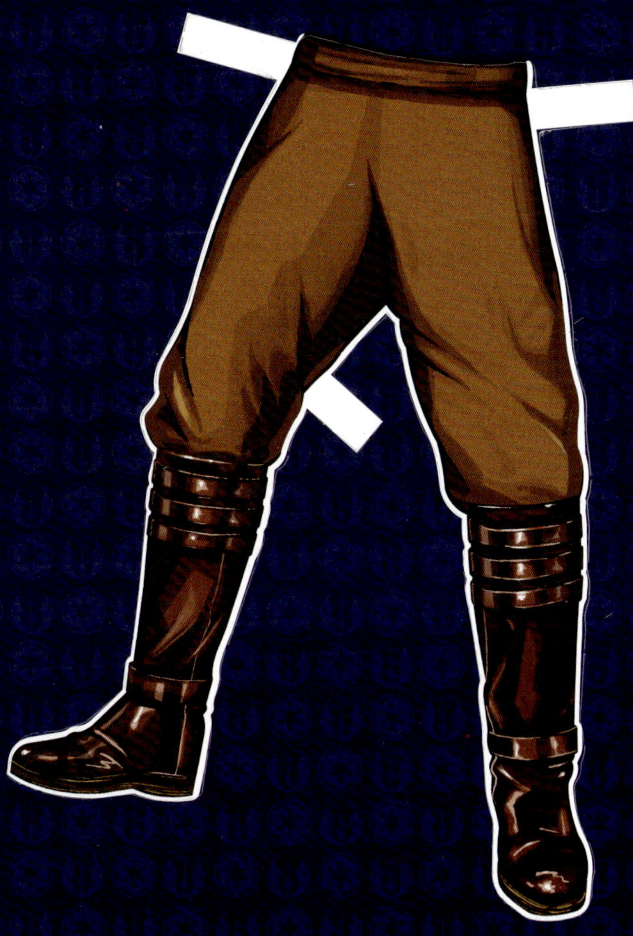

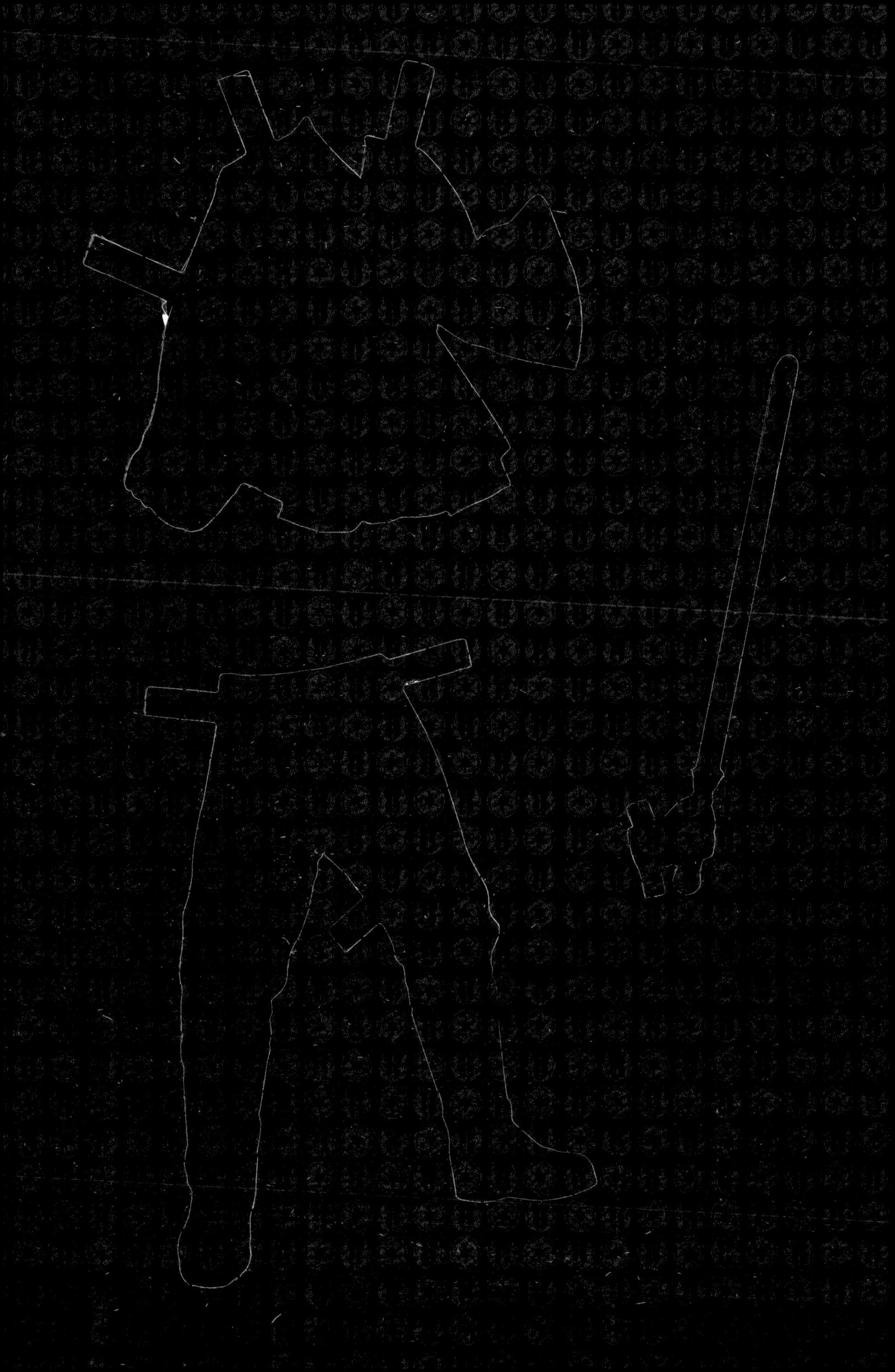

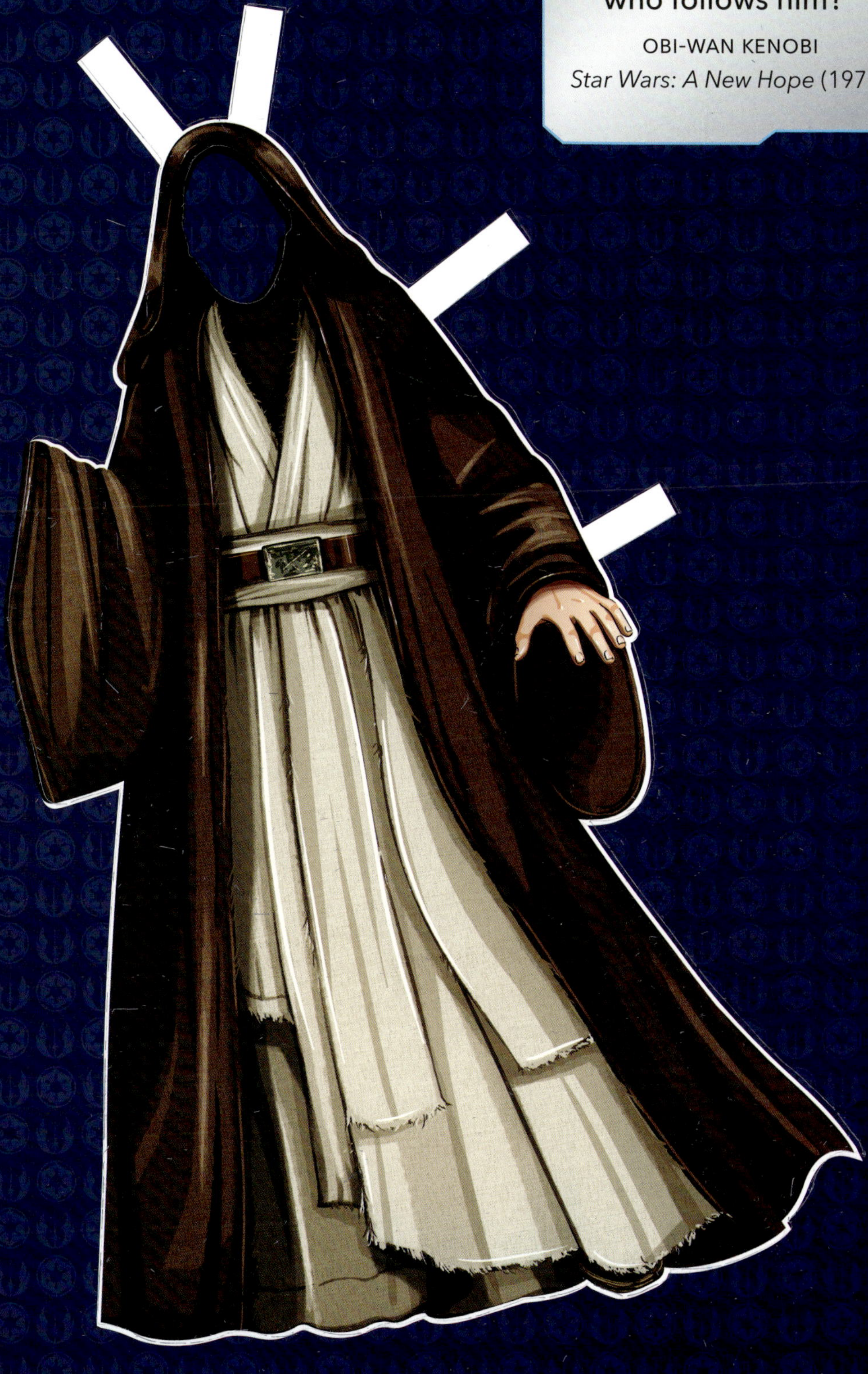

"Who's more foolish? The fool or the fool who follows him?"

OBI-WAN KENOBI
Star Wars: A New Hope (1977)

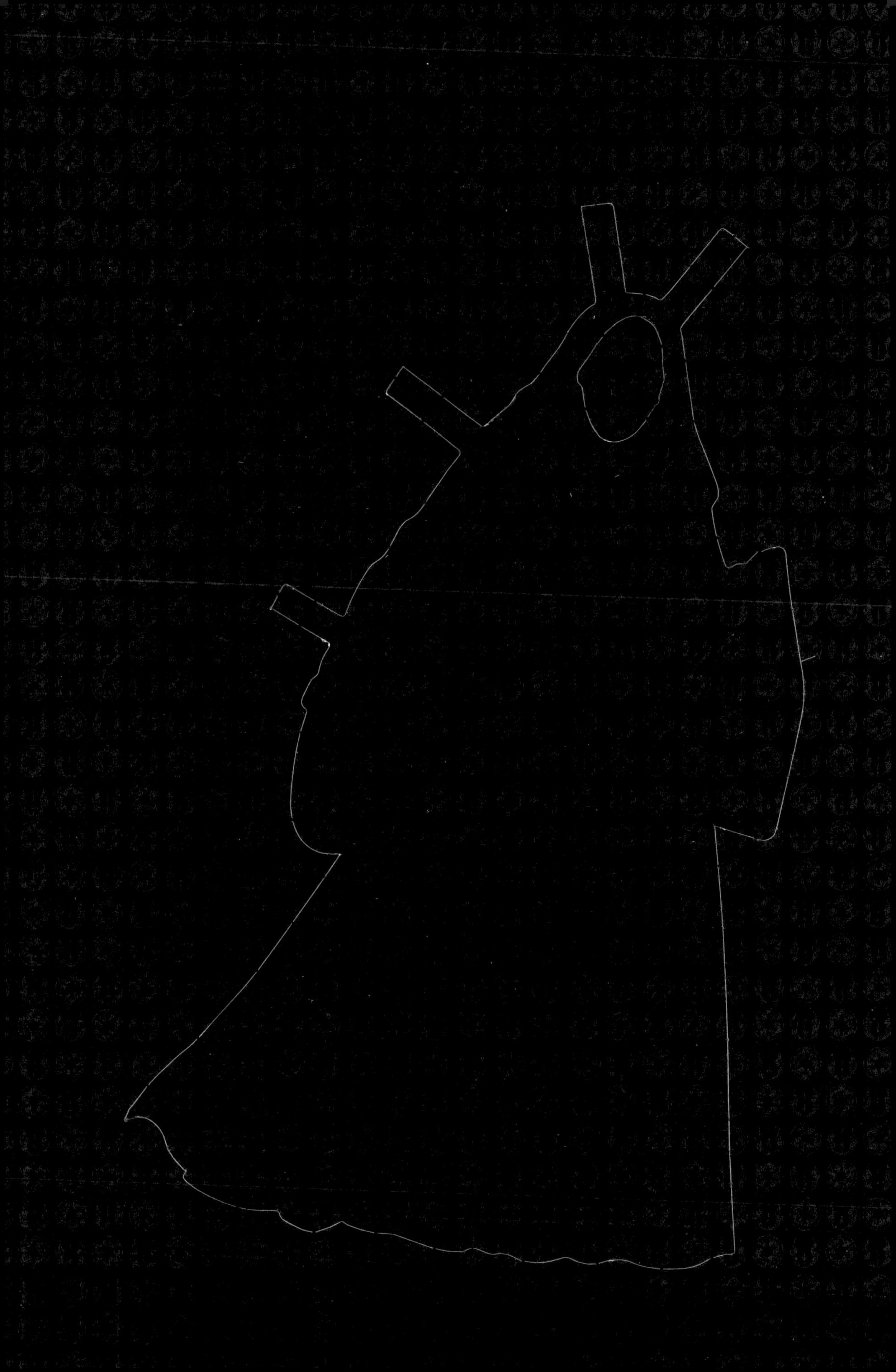

REY SKYWALKER

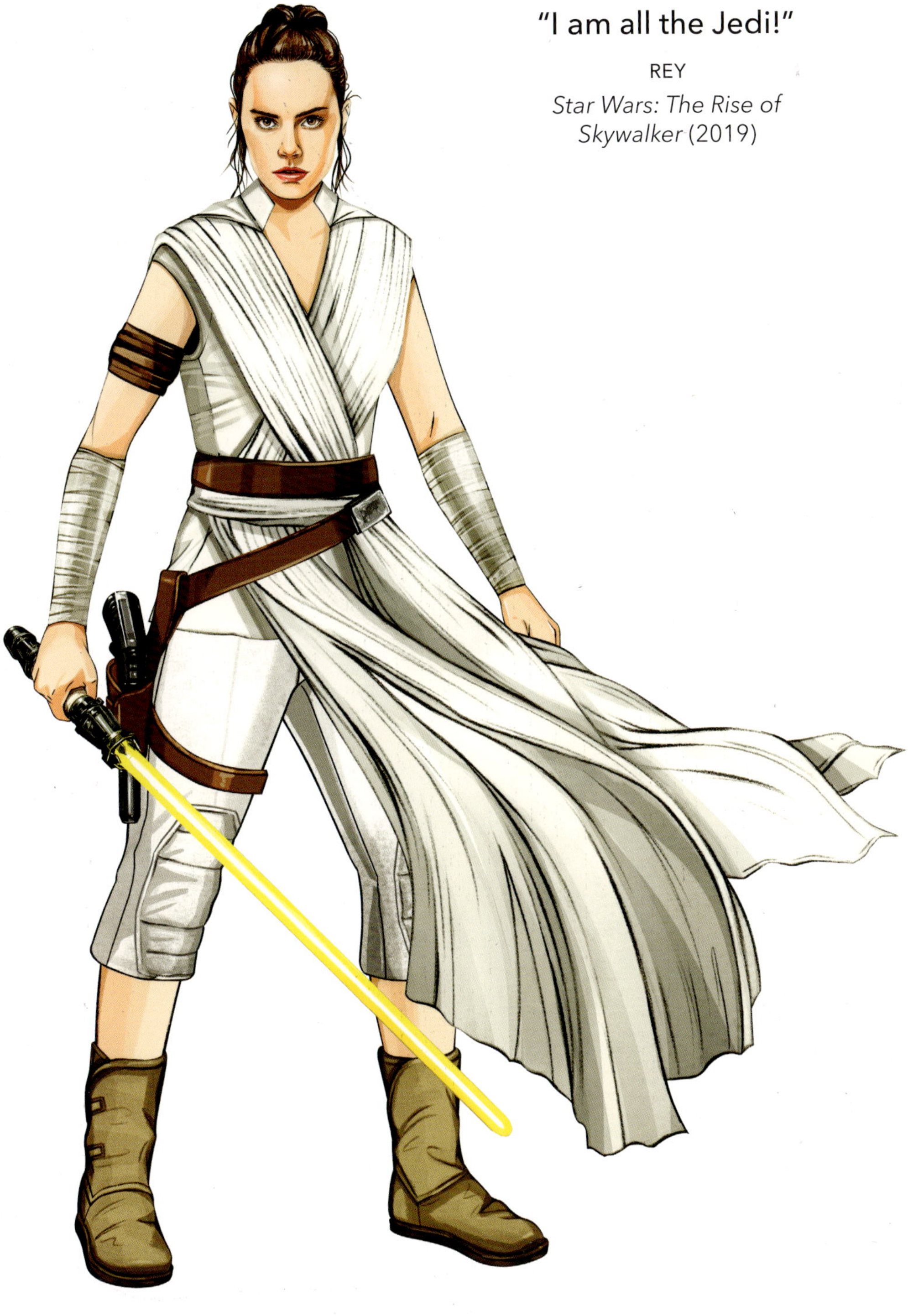

"I am all the Jedi!"

REY

Star Wars: The Rise of Skywalker (2019)

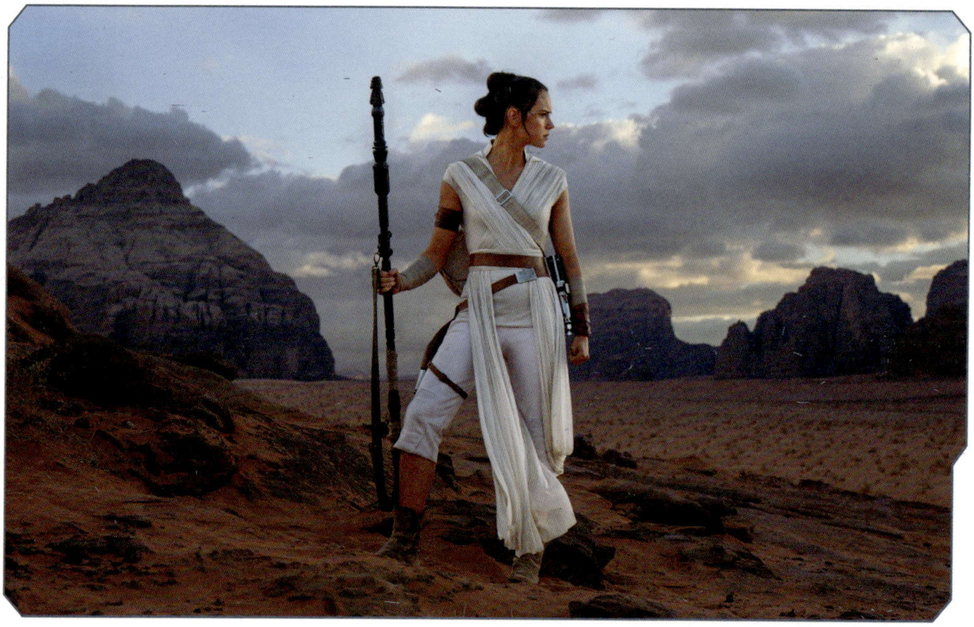

In 2015, *Star Wars* fans were rewarded with an all-new trilogy that picks up decades after the events of 1983's *Star Wars: Return of the Jedi*. Original trilogy stars Mark Hamill (Luke Skywalker), Carrie Fisher (Princess Leia), and Harrison Ford (Han Solo) returned alongside new characters to expand the mythology of the galaxy far, far away. Perhaps the most mysterious newcomer was a young woman known as Rey, portrayed by actress Daisy Ridley.

When we first encounter Rey in *Star Wars: The Force Awakens*, she's a scavenger on the desert planet Jakku. She teams up with former stormtrooper Finn, becomes enmeshed with the Resistance (led by now-General Leia) and fights against the sinister First Order, and takes her first sensitive steps toward learning about the Force. The earthen hues of Rey's clothing in *Star Wars: The Force Awakens* evoke the garb Luke Skywalker wears on Tatooine. Both characters are dressed in lightweight but durable clothing that is suited to a harsh desert environment. As Rey explores her connection to the Force over subsequent films and meets Luke Skywalker, her wardrobe begins to take on a Jedi look, with a hood and draped cloths, while still echoing her traditional wardrobe. The crisp white color also shows a shared connection with Leia and Padmé before her.

The goggles that Rey wears in *Star Wars: The Force Awakens* are lenses from a stormtrooper helmet.

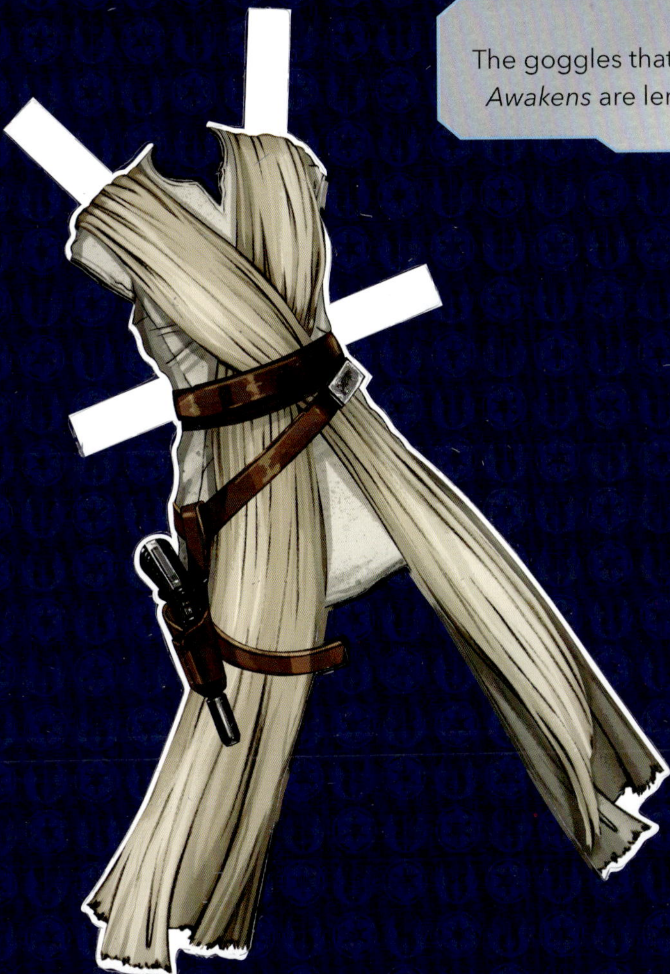

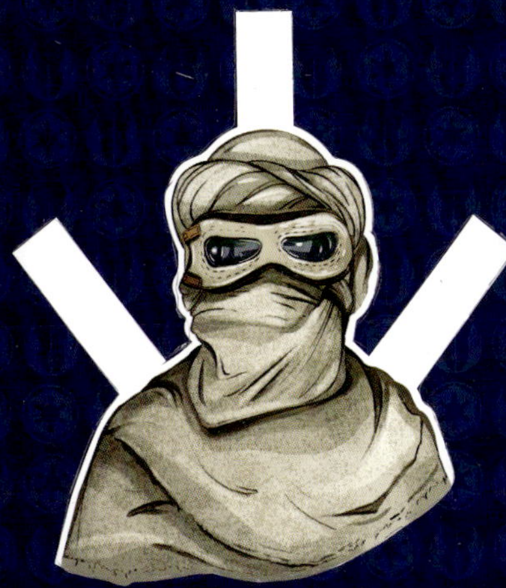

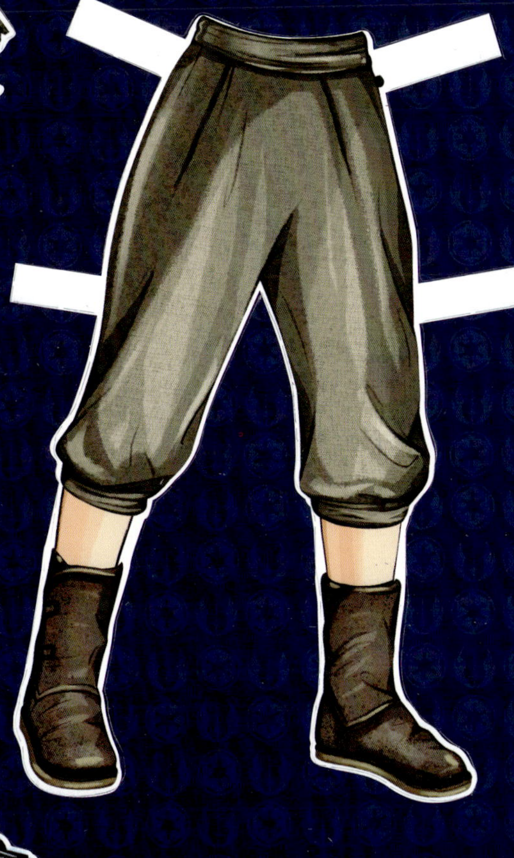

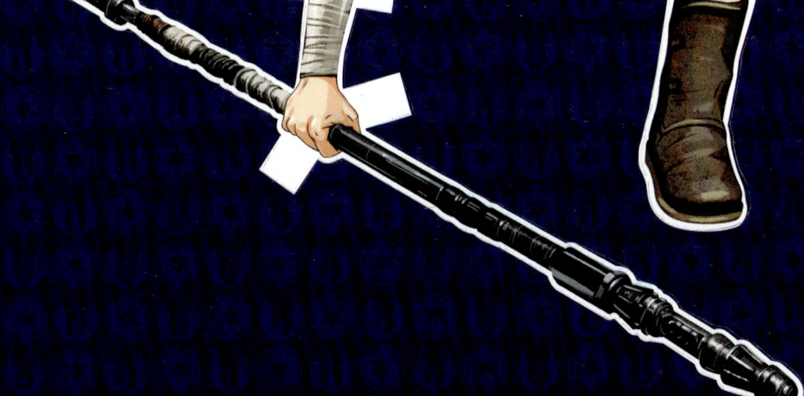

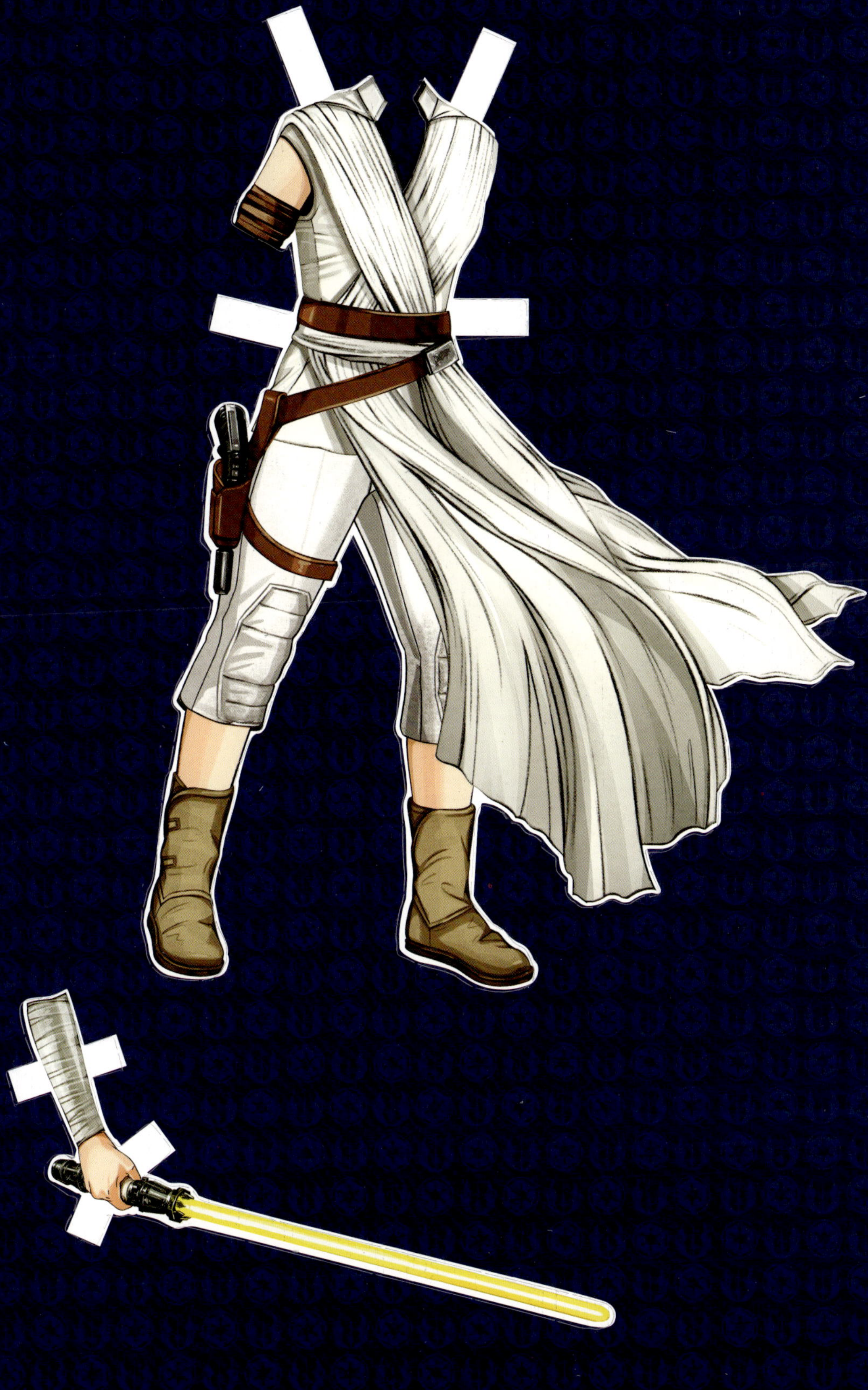

FINN

"... I'm done with the First Order. I'm never going back."

FINN

Star Wars: The Force Awakens (2015)

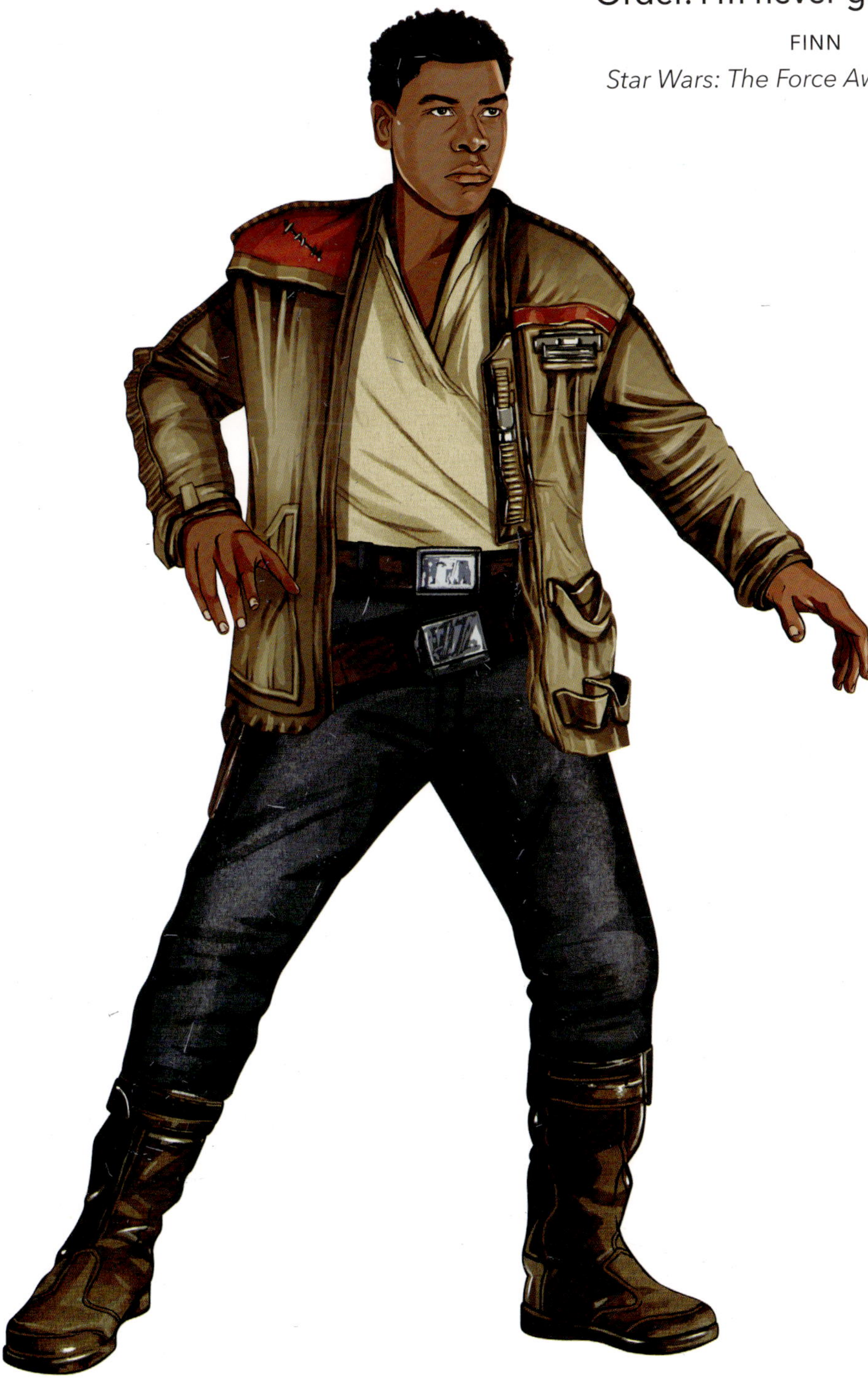

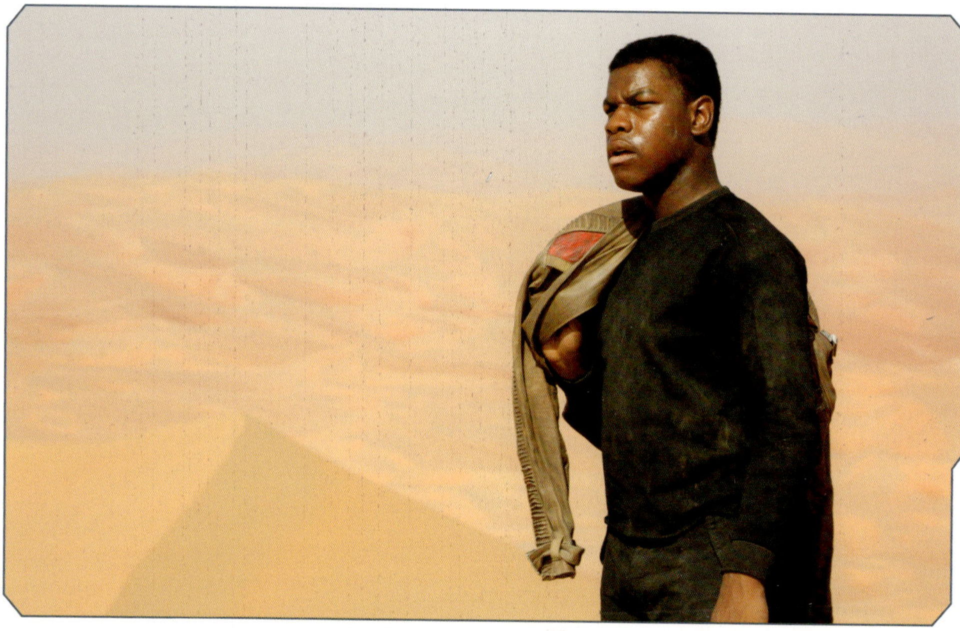

From the moment he first removes his helmet in 2015's *Star Wars: The Force Awakens*, gasping for air, stormtrooper FN-2187–or Finn, as he comes to be known–proves to be unlike any character seen before in the epic saga. Finn witnesses firsthand the cruel violence of the evil First Order as it inflicts pain and suffering on a small village on the planet Jakku. As a stormtrooper, Finn is expected to participate, yet he refuses to fire his weapon. Thus begins Finn's heroic journey as he struggles to follow his conscience and renounce the First Order–and ultimately joins the Resistance to fight alongside Rey.

Finn first appears dressed in full stormtrooper body armor. As the foot soldiers of the Empire in the original trilogy, stormtroopers serve much the same role in the First Order. That iconic look impressed actor John Boyega the first time he donned the stormtrooper costume; he felt that in many ways, it was the final step in becoming his character.

Finn is much more than a stormtrooper, though. He grows disillusioned with the First Order and comes to understand that he must join the Resistance and fight to save what's good in the galaxy. No longer clad in the armor of a stormtrooper, the new Finn wears the flight jacket of Resistance pilot Poe Dameron. His look takes on almost a Han Solo-ish quality, becoming more rugged as he transitions from "just a number" in the First Order to a key and independent player in the galactic fight for freedom.

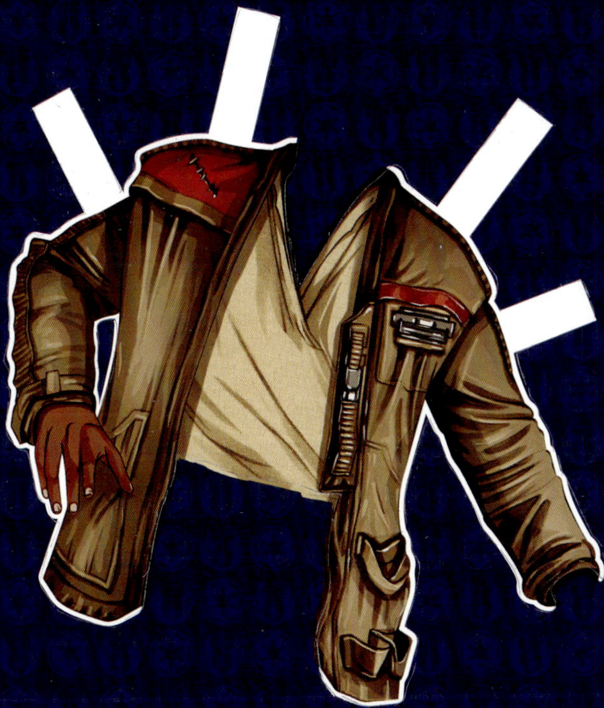

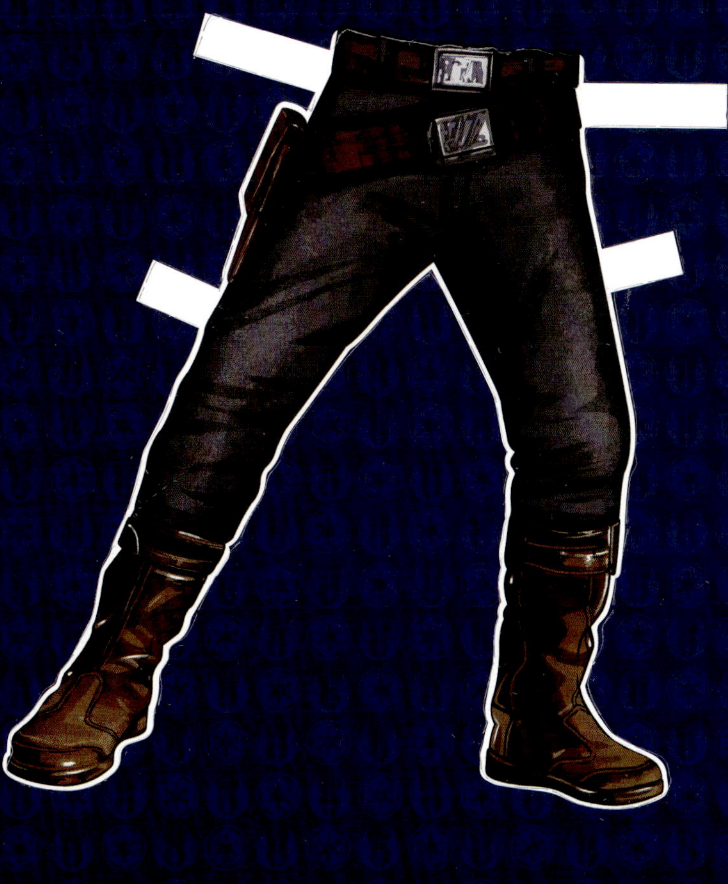

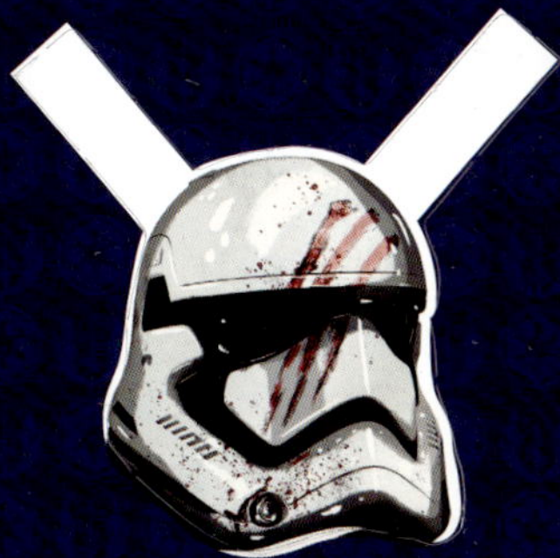

The sleeker look for the First Order stormtrooper armor in *Star Wars: The Force Awakens* plays to a hard, white, plastic-like concept, evolving from the look of the Empire's stormtroopers in the original trilogy.

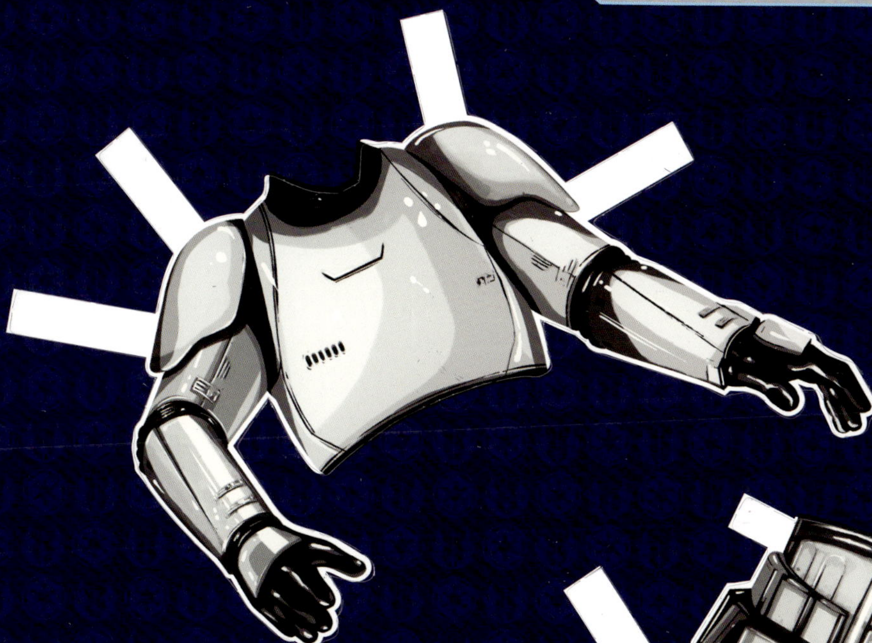

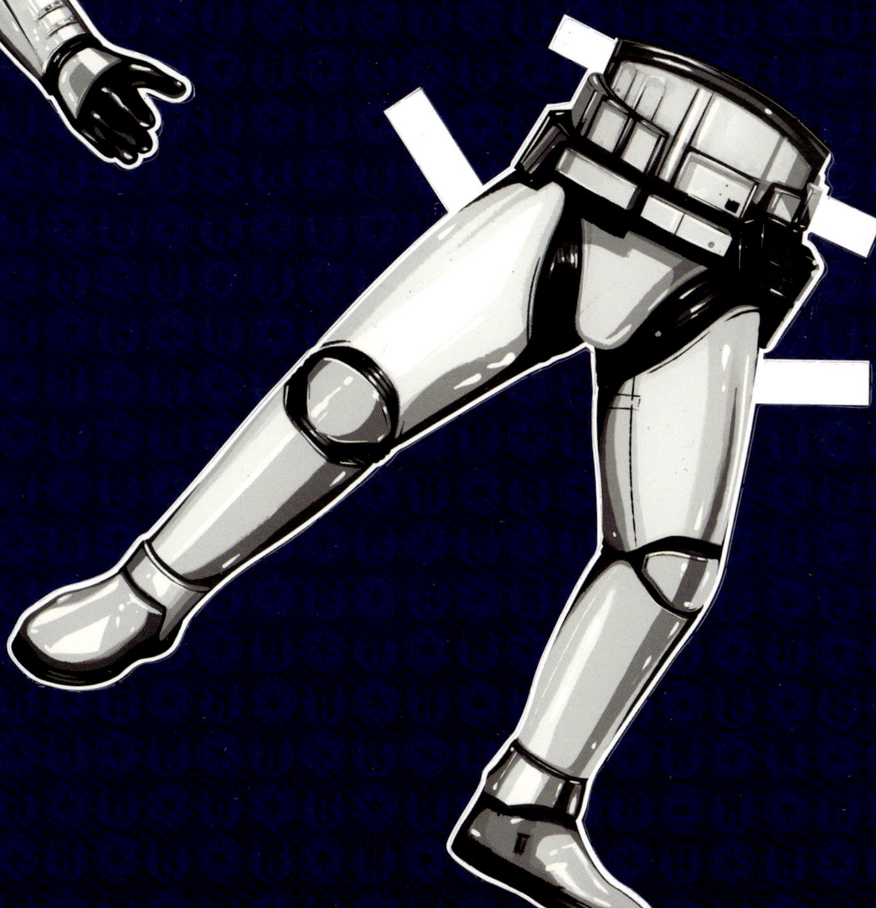